THE GREATEST DA VINCI DEAL

HOW RUSSIA ENSNARED DONALD TRUMP WITH THE WORLD'S
MOST EXPENSIVE PAINTING AND PRIVATE RESIDENCE,
DMITRY RYBOLOVLEV, YVES BOUVIER AND FREEPORTS

Yuri Felshtinsky

GIBSON SQUARE

This edition first published by Gibson Square in the US only

rights@gibsonsquare.com

www.gibsonsquare.com

Papers used by Gibson Square are natural, recyclable products made from wood grown in sustainable forests; inks used are vegetable based. Manufacturing conforms to ISO 14001, and is accredited to FSC and PEFC chain of custody schemes. Color-printing is through a certified CarbonNeutral® company that offsets its CO2 emissions.

CONTENTS

Salvator Mundi

This story began a long time ago. On 15 April 1452, named Leonardo Da Vinci was born in the settlement of Anchiano near the hill town of Vinci in the Republic of Florence. He is famous for painting the Mona Lisa, one of the world's greatest masterpieces.

Today, his name is known for one more reason: on 15 November 2017, the painting on wood attributed to him and called *Salvator Mundi* (*Savior of the World*) was purchased through Christie's Auction House in New York by the Crown Prince of Saudi Arabia Mohammed bin Salman for the record price of $450,312,500. To be specific: according to the opinion of many experts, Da Vinci himself could have painted just a small part of the painting, maybe one-tenth of it. The rest was painted later. Therefore, it is not surprising that Christie's, to be on the safe side, included the following statement in its pre-auction announcement: "Unlike Leonardo's other works *Salvator Mundi* is missing azurite, used as an underpainting in all of Leonardo's other paintings."

Can such a painting be considered a Da Vinci painting?

Yves Bouvier, who sold this painting to the work's penultimate owner, Dmitry Rybolovlev, gave this answer in August 2023: "Imagine buying an antique car for your collection, but can it be considered an antique if it only has a steering wheel and a chair from that era and everything else is modern? That's exactly the question."

On 15 November 2017, in the Christie's auction building in New York, the bidders addressed a completely different question, which has little to do with Da Vinci or art: someone paid another for the *Salvator Mundi*. It remains for us to understand to whom and by whom?

Let us start from the beginning. A day before the auction, a Saudi, Prince Bader bin Abdullah bin Mohammed bin Farhan Al Saud, came forward as a potential buyer, placing a guaranteed bid of $100 million to participate in the auction. This was the minimum amount determined for all the auction participants after the guarantee buyer agreed to pay $100 million.

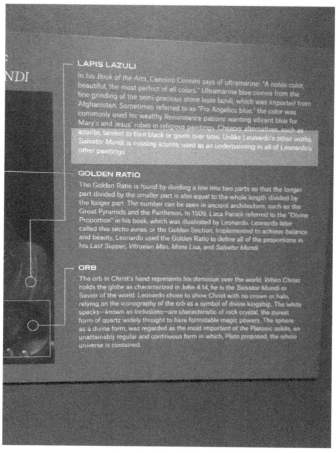

The signage shown inside the Christies showroom next to the painting and before the auction: "Unlike Leonardo's other works Salvator Mundi is missing azurite, used as an underpainting in all of Leonardo's other paintings."

After the bidding closed, Christie's tried to conceal the identity of the buyer for as long as possible. But journalists soon discovered it soon enough. On 6 December 2017, it was reported that the painting was purchased through Prince Bader by Crown Prince Mohammed bin Salman.

Well, he purchased it and immediately gave it away as a present to a museum in Abu Dhabi—the capital of the United Arab Emirates (UAE)[1].

Curiously, at that time, the Crown Prince hardly had time to spare to devote to auction-hunting for Renaissance art. On 4 November (11 days before the auction), he staged a daring *coup d'état* in Saudi Arabia, arresting 200 of his relatives who held important government posts. Holding them in the Riyadh Ritz Carlton, the detainees were interrogated and forced to give testimony (according to some, even through the use of torture). Yet, it seems to have been at the top of his agenda to purchase in New York a painting depicting Jesus Christ through one of the few remaining loyal relatives and to present it to a neighboring country.

However, we were going to start right from the beginning.

1

The Rise of Dmitry Rybolovlev, Oligarch

The vendor at Christies of *Salvator Mundi*, Dmitry Rybolovlev, was born on 22 November 1966, in Perm. Rybolovlev was a highly educated man from an intellectual family. A doctor, he graduated from the Perm Medical Institute where his father Evgeny Rybolovlev, a well-known cardiologist, was a professor.

On 24 July 1987, Rybolovlev married 21-year-old Elena Chuprakova, daughter of Valery Chuprakov, director of the Perm mineral water plant. Rybolovlev met Elena at university. They had two daughters. Ekaterina was born in 1989 and Anna in 2001.

After the collapse of the Soviet Union, he, along with many others, became an entrepreneur working with his father in the wholesale trade of medical supplies. In the spring of 1992, he temporarily moved to Moscow, where he obtained a broker's certificate from the Ministry of Finance of the Russian Federation, which gave him the right to work with securities—an innovation at the time.

Just like many others, he had difficulty conducting his business in post-USSR Russia. This was because one had to deal with criminals, and had become a criminal. The Russian government officials in the Prosecutor's Office (which was the same office as the one formerly under the auspices of the Soviet government) considered everyone conducting business success-fully in those murky times as *prima facie* criminals and initiated criminal pro-ceedings constantly. It was genuinely challenging to determine who was and who was not a real criminal, rather than what used to be termed an 'enemy of the people'.

The story of Roman Abramovich, a rising businessman and, in this sense, Rybolovlev's peer, was illustrative. On 9 June 1992, criminal proceedings were initiated in Moscow against Abramovich, alleging that he stole 55 tankers with diesel fuel. Ten days later, the public prosecutor ordered his arrest since Abramovich, in their opinion, "constituted a flight risk and prevented the restoration of justice".

We know the outcome of this 1992 criminal trial against Abramovich. Many years later he purchased the Chelsea Football Club and moved to the UK. After the full-scale war started by Russia to attack Ukraine in 2022, however, the UK government started making inquiries regarding the source of Abramovich's wealth and he was forced to sell Chelsea and leave the UK.

Rybolovlev's career followed a similar oligarch trajectory. He built his business in Perm in 1993-1996 surrounded by gangsters for protection. In those years, the former USSR had the "sale of the century". Virtually all state property—and everything in the USSR was state property—was now subject to "privatization", and the Russian government was keen for this "privatization" to take place as soon as possible so that the former Soviet state could not be resurrected and control again the country's economy. To privatize enterprises, "auctions" were held. Formally speaking, anyone could participate in the auctions: private citizens, companies, the enterprises themselves... These enterprises were bought with a specially created new currency—"vouchers" issued by the government free of charge to every Russian person. In other words, Russia was valued at a certain amount, this amount was divided by the number of Russian citizens, and everyone got their private share of the pie, or everything previously held by the state on behalf of the Russian people as a monopolist. With this share, it was possible to purchase a share in a single enterprise. The majority of Russians didn't understand the new system and sold their shares on, however, considering them as worthless as the ex-USSR itself. To buy an entire enterprise or a substantial share of it, you simply had to buy a lot of vouchers.

This is exactly what Rybolovlev did. In 1993, to participate in auctions of state-owned enterprises in the Perm region, Rybolovlev created and became the general director of the Stone Belt Voucher Investment Fund, an organization that collected, bought, and reinvested privatization vouchers. Money was needed to buy up vouchers. Nobody had any money of their own. It was necessary to take loans from new commercial banks and sign partnership agreements with them on transferring to the banks the shares in enterprises privatized with the bank's money.

Rybolovlev managed to create his bank in Perm—Credit FD Bank[2]. The bank was created thanks to the fact that the most powerful Perm enterprises agreed to be shareholders of the bank and allowed all their cash flows and payments to be channeled through the bank. Rybolovlev became the general director of the bank. On 29 June 1994, Vladimir Shevtsov, deputy chairman of the Perm Regional State Property Fund and the regional branch of the State Privatization Agency, became deputy general director of Credit FD Bank. Both Rybolovlev and Shevtsov became members of the bank's board of directors. As Shevtsov later recounted, he "was responsible for the technical side of the bank's activities and for the security service", while "Rybolovlev was responsible for all activities related to finance, the stock market and the securities market."

Rybolovlev's first privatization experience was the 1993 privatization of a margarine factory in Perm, which was conducted through the Stone Belt Voucher Investment Fund by Vladimir Nelyubin, who was not yet known to Rybolovlev. Nelyubin was a local businessman with criminal connections and had repeatedly served prison terms for extortion.

After the first successful privatization of a margarine factory, the relationship between Rybolovlev and Nelyubin became close. Rybolovlev accepted from him large sums of "dirty" money collected through extortion and used this money to buy stakes in the privatized companies. In return, Nelyubin and his associates (by verbal agreement) received a percentage of the privatized businesses and a monopoly on trading contracts in the regional market.

Rybolovlev invested not his own money in tenders and auctions, but the funds of the plant or company whose shares were bought. For example, in 1993 Neftekhimik Company signed an agreement with the private investment fund Stone Belt to buy back shares from its employees and transferred RUB 1 billion to Stone Belt. However, the purchased shares were not transferred to Neftekhimik Company but became part of a more complex exchange that by mid-1994 had bought up shares in Metafrax Company, Azot Company, and Stone Belt itself. All of this was done with a billion from Neftekhimik, which became both a shareholder in Rybolovlev's Credit FD Bank and a shareholder in the companies being bought up.

In the privatization projects, the functions were divided. Rybolovlev was in charge of finance and took over negotiations with the CEO of the company being privatized, who—not disinterestedly—helped to reduce the starting price of the auction as much as possible. Nelyubin made sure that no competitors from Moscow, Perm, or other cities appeared at the auction, so that the auction would not become an auction, and it would be possible, having preliminarily eliminated the competitors, to buy a stake in the enterprise at the starting price "in the absence of participation of other bidders". Rybolovlev passed information to Nelyubin by telephone about various bids for participation in auctions for the privatization of Perm enterprises, and Nelyubin "by the method of persuasion" ensured that Muscovites refused to participate in these auctions, involving, if necessary, his gangsters, who explained to competitors in "plain language" that they should not fight for the shares of this or another company. For this (by verbal agreement) Nelyubin received a part of the company's shares and the right to sell the company's products on the domestic market.

In addition, at the first stage, Nelyubin helped Rybolovlev with the purchase of privatization vouchers for Uralkali, which used the vouchers to buy shares in various Perm companies, including Uralkali itself.

The business began to expand. Rybolovlev's new gangster partners in Perm were Victor Chernyavsky, Oleg Lomakin, and Sergei Makarov, who, as Vadim Efimov, a member of the gang, said in 1995, "helped Rybolovlev to buy shares." As the General Director of Azot Company, M.A. Petruniak, later recalled, "[a]ccess to the auctions was closed to representatives of large Moscow companies with a large number of vouchers, which allowed Rybolovlev to acquire large blocks of shares" at very low prices.

The partnership with gangsters brought fruitful results: during the privatization of Sylvinit, Rybolovlev managed to acquire just 1% of shares at auction before the involvement of bandits. When the bandits were brought in, he acquired 39%. Rybolovlev worked under their patronage, and they also provided him with "physical protection from competitors" (as described by one of the managers of Neftekhimik).

Rybolovlev's cooperation with Oleg Lomakin, which played a fatal role in Rybolovlev's life, began in 1993-1994 when they agreed to jointly buy shares in several companies, including Neftekhimik. Rybolovlev set up a department to buy shares on the secondary market and, including Nelyubin as a partner, borrowed RUB 100 million from two financial institutions they had set up: Credit FD Bank and the investment company Financial House. The money was invested first in the purchase of vouchers and then in shares of Neftekhimik, where V.M. Kazantsev was the general director at the time.

There was a verbal agreement between Rybolovlev and the management of Neftekhimik that they would sell approximately 19% of the company's shares to Stone Belt. At the same time, the money to buy these shares was transferred from Neftekhimik's accounts at Credit FD Bank. In other words, Stone Belt bought the company's shares with the company's own money, and as a result, it bought 19.75% of the shares, intending to continue buying up Neftekhimik's shares in the hope of gaining a controlling stake. At the same time, the shares themselves remained with Rybolovlev as a private individual, not with Stone Belt, which paid for the shares with Neftekhimik's money.

Rybolovlev's "cover" (in Russian, "*krysha*", or "roof") in Moscow (according to many people in Rybolovlev's entourage, including his partners) was the well-known criminal authority Seifeddin Rustamov (aka "Rustam", aka "Ruslan"), a wrestler and master of sports who had lived in Perm for 13 years before leaving for Moscow. He specialized in neutralizing possible competitors in advance of auctions by various means.

Rustamov was the only person whom Rybolovlev truly respected, listened to, and feared at the same time. "Ruslan—a powerful structure, an authority, and the guys will not argue with him", "this is a powerful criminal cover", "a criminal authority," "and others will respect and fulfill his decisions"—this is a selection of Rybolovlev's statements about Rustamov. All the other bandits (Rybolovlev's partners) also treated Rustamov with respect, recognizing him as a "criminal authority."

While Rustamov and Nelyubin solved "problems" in Moscow, Chernyavsky, Makarov and Lomakin solved "problems" that arose at the local level—in Perm—by preventing competitors from entering the auctions by all legal and illegal means. Chernyavsky's role in privatization and buying up shares was also that he, having received information about the participants of auctions in Perm, entered into a tacit agreement on the division of the market: some corporations would buy shares of some enterprises, and other corporations would buy shares of others so that there would be no competition and no real auctions.

It is very important to understand that all the agreements were oral. All shares were bought in Rybolovlev's name. However, no agreements or documents on the division of these shares were signed. Everything was based on a handshake and a word of honor, on "concepts", rather than legal arrangements. For Russia in the 1990s, this way of concluding agreements was generally accepted and even prevailed. But this could not but lead sooner or later to misunderstandings and conflicts, often ending in the murder of one or another of the partners in a common business. Times were brutal and bloody.

At the latest in March-April 1994, when the privatization of the Perm enterprises was just beginning, the participants in the deal to privatize the chemical and petrochemical enterprises of the Perm region, who met regularly in Rybolovlev's office at Credit FD, agreed that the shares they were buying would be divided equally between Rybolovlev (50%) and "everyone else" (50%). "All others" (Chernyavsky, Nelyubin, Makarov, and Lomakin) shared the remaining 50% equally among themselves.

Under this scheme, Rybolovlev acquired his first stake in several privatized companies in the industry through his Stone Belt. The shares were registered in the name of Rybolovlev's structures, which multiplied. But the gangsters knew and believed that the shares belonged to them all together, especially since many of them, as well as Rybolovlev's men, were put on the boards of directors of the companies being privatized. Shevtsov, Rybolovlev's partner in Credit FD Bank, was a member of the board of directors of Metafrax, Uralkali, Sylvinit, and Credit FD Bank until the late 2000s. Nelyubin, as a representative of Credit FD Bank, became a member of the board of directors of Metafrax JSC.

Rybolovlev was pressured to rewrite the share certificates of Uralkali, Metafrax, Azot, and Neftekhimik to his partners as individuals or to "sell" them to LIPS LLP, a new structure established on a parity basis by Chernyavsky, Lomakin, Makarov, Nelyubin, and Rustamov. It was all about the same 50% of Rybolovlev's shares. But "Rybolovlev," according to Efimov, "did not want to divide the shares," and each time he gave "many arguments as to why the share ownership should not be transferred," thereby violating "the terms of the existing verbal agreements."

Rybolovlev's partners, for their part, kept coming back to this issue, arguing, as Shevtsov said, that "it is necessary to divide the shares bought at the auctions, because they [the bandits] helped organize the auctions and participated in them", and the shares later bought by Rybolovlev "on the secondary market" were purchased with common money, and therefore were also subject to division. "Rybolovlev tried not to respond to these requests,"—Shevtsov recalled. After "prolonged psychological pressure" from Chernyavsky, Nelyubin, Makarov, and Lomakin, Rybolovlev agreed to transfer to them 5% of Uralkali, 10% of Methanol, and 8% of Neftekhimik. In February 1995, 15% of the shares of JSCB Credit FD owned by Neftekhimik were sold to LIPS. Nelyubin and Makarov were made members of the bank's Board of Directors, and Lomakin became a shareholder of the bank.

In addition, Rybolovlev was constantly being asked for "small loans for the construction of personal houses", letters were brought asking for money "for charitable purposes", for the development of sports and horse breeding, for the organization of a tournament in memory of the famous Russian wrestler Ivan Poddubny. At one point, Rybolovlev and Shevtsov had said that "the bank is not a cash cow" and refused to extend any more money. "After this refusal to provide funds for sports propaganda, relations with Nelyubin became unpleasant," Shevtsov recalled.

But from the gangsters' point of view, these were all small handouts, far from the original 50% agreement. At one point Chernyavsky told Rybolovlev that they were a "criminal cover" for his companies and Rybolovlev would "be forced to split the shares anyway."

As early as 1993, Rybolovlev hired personal guards. By 1995 he had twelve of them. He ordered to constantly change his route when he got a lift, not to leave cars unattended, to check the elevators and the lobby of the building Rybolovlev was entering," one of his bodyguards recalled. Then Rybolovlev started wearing a bulletproof vest. Then he bought himself an armored car. The bags of all people entering his office were checked by security guards. At times he had to go into hiding, including travel abroad.

In 1994 Rybolovlev decided to obtain a controlling stake in Neftekhimik. Accordingly, in January 1995, he replaced Kazantsev, who was disloyal to him and who, in Rybolovlev's words, "sold them out," with E.N. Panteleimonov. With Panteleimonov he hoped to find a common language.

To prevent Rybolovlev and his group from obtaining a controlling stake in Neftekhimik, Kazantsev sold part of Neftekhimik's shares to Permstroy

Bank and Solvalub Financial Group, rather than to Rybolovlev. The Moscow-based Solvalub also wanted a controlling stake in Neftekhimik and bought up 20.95% of the shares at that time, becoming the main competitor of Rybolovlev and Credit FD Bank. As a result, Solvalub, as part of the division of markets between partners, began to fully control the export market of Neftekhimik, which was the most profitable one.

It is understandable that after this "betrayal," Rybolovlev decided to change the general director of Neftekhimik to a person loyal to him and starting in November 1994, he repeatedly offered Kazantsev to leave his post voluntarily, but Kazantsev refused every time. It was virtually impossible to remove the general director against his will at Neftekhimik. According to the company's charter, the general director was elected for two years and could not be removed before the expiration of that term. And to change the charter it was necessary to get a two-thirds majority of the shareholders' votes, which was unattainable: neither the company's shareholders nor the staff working at the plant, who had the right to vote, would go for it.

To force Kazantsev to resign, in December 1994, during Kazantsev's absence, a financial audit of the company was conducted, which concluded that Kazantsev's actions as general director had caused Neftekhimik a loss of RUB 8 billion. Kazantsev cross-checked the financial audit report and proved that as a result of his activities as CEO, the company made a profit of RUB 6 million and that the audit data had been fabricated by Rybolovlev's men. "I am no longer responsible for your safety,"— Rybolovlev told Kazantsev by telephone, which was a blatant threat to physically eliminate his adversary.

Also in December 1994, Shevtsov suggested that A.I. Krechetov "inflict bodily harm on Kazantsev.. so that he resigns" because "he was unwilling to cooperate and was getting in the way."

Krechetov worked in Rybolovlev's system as a security guard at Rybolovlev's and Shevtsov's bank offices for a salary of $300 per month. He had previously served in the Special Forces in Kazakhstan, guarding facilities of special importance, was skilled in all types of weapons, and was a master of sport in boxing. After leaving the army, he worked as an instructor in unarmed combat, then took bodyguard courses and even got a diploma as an electronic engineer.

Krechetov had already started looking for people to beat up Kazantsev, but at the end of December 1994, the assignment was canceled as Kazantsev had agreed to resign and signed a resignation letter on 10 January 1995, dated 21 January. On 23 January 1995, Panteleimonov assumed the duties of general director, and in April 1995, a shareholders' meeting was held and the shareholders confirmed their approval of his candidature by a vote.

After Rybolovlev became co-owner of Metafrax in 1995, he traveled for the first time to Geneva, where Metafrax had a branch, and applied for a Swiss residence permit as an employee of Metafrax. As Rybolovlev's wife recalled much later, "[i]n 1994, following the privatization of many Russian companies, our family was being threatened by Russian criminals as a consequence of Dmitry's increased success in his business activities. Dmitry and I had many discussions about the need to move out of Russia and possible locations where we could set up our household and still allow Dmitry to conduct his business... He decided that Geneva would be a safe place to live given what was happening in Russia during the period of privatization. Once Dmitry's residency permit was granted, we decided to set up our home in Geneva... and did so in May 1995."

But now only Elena and their daughter Yekaterina lived permanently in Geneva. Rybolovlev himself spent most of his time in Russia. It seems that it was during this period that Rybolovlev decided to "dump" his gangsters—all but one of them,—Rustamov. He decided to replace the Perm gangster "roof" with a "Moscow" one.

Negotiations on this issue between Rybolovlev and Ruslan, on the one hand, and Chernyavsky, Lomakin, Nelyubin, and Makarov, on the other, were held in Moscow in the summer of 1995. "We are parting with them,"— Rybolovlev told M.V. Oschepkov, head of his security service at the time, referring to Chernyavsky, Nelyubin, Makarov, and Lomakin. The bandits realized that "Rybolovlev wanted to share everything with Ruslan". Lomakin, according to Rybolovlev, was told that he had "nothing more to do in Neftekhimik."

Rustamov believed that he had agreed on everything with his Perm brethren. On 4 August 1995, the new director of Neftekhimik, Panteleimonov, at Rybolovlev's call, flew to Moscow to meet with Rustamov and coordinate financial matters with him. After meeting and discussing everything, Panteleimonov realized that "Ruslan supports Rybolovlev, and the guys (Nelyubin, Chernyavsky, Lomakin) are 'leaving'". Now Neftekhimik had to pay Rustamov directly, and Rustamov guaranteed Rybolovlev and Panteleimonov no trouble. The first money from the account of one of Rybolovlev's companies was transferred to Rustamov in the first half of August. At the same time, the main money from the joint activities of the businesses in which Rybolovlev was a shareholder began to be transferred to the Moscow branch of Credit FD. Rustamov himself was appointed deputy director of the Moscow branch and assistant sales manager of Credit FD. It seems that he also received 10% in Rybolovlev's companies. At the same time, the Perm bandits were removed from the bank's board of directors.

On 4 September 1995, Panteleimonov was shot dead at the entrance of his house in Perm.

As Panteleimonov's wife was telling, that morning her husband was going to go to a business meeting. At 7.55 a.m. he left the flat to walk the dog, and immediately the wife "heard a popping sound". She ran out onto the landing and saw her husband lying on the floor. According to her, "he had no conflicts with anyone and did not expect an attack on himself".

On 18 March 1996, the police detained Lomakin and Yuri Kirsanov on suspicion of involvement in the murder. But it was a completely different murder: on the night of 8 November 1995, a member of Lomakin's criminal group, D.G. Zuev, was killed.

Here it is very appropriate to emphasize that Rybolovlev's partner Oleg Gennadievich Lomakin was a classic gangster and headed a gang of robbers and murderers he had assembled. He was a former "Afghan", i.e., a man who had been through the war in Afghanistan, had participated in combat operations, and knew how to handle weapons, even a grenade launcher. Some of his acquaintances expressed the opinion that in Afghanistan he had "lost his mind" and became uncontrollable. In 1989, Lomakin was sentenced to five years under a criminal article. In 1992 he was "paroled". But on the afternoon of 22 December 1992, he got into an argument at the Central Market in Perm with a taxi driver who refused to drive him for the offered RUB 200 (the taxi driver asked for RUB 500, and the ruble exchange rate was about RUB 400 per $1) and shot him in the face with a gas pistol, which he had no right to carry. Lomakin rushed to flee the market but was detained. He was jailed again but was soon released. In 1993-1994, he somehow became Rybolovlev's partner in the privatization of chemical and petrochemical enterprises in the Perm region, although Rybolovlev could not have been unaware that Lomakin was a criminal and a creasy.

It is possible that another Lomakin played a role in bringing Rybolovlev and Oleg Gennadievich Lomakin together: Anatoly Gennadievich Lomakin, although nowhere in his biography is it stated that he was O.G. Lomakin's brother.

A. G. Lomakin was born in 1952. In 1975 he graduated from the prestigious and hard-to-get-in Moscow State Institute of International Relations (MGIMO). Until 1985, he worked in one of the divisions of Soyuzpromexport, where he rose to the position of Director of the enterprise "Potassium Agrokhimexport". Then he worked in the Trade Representation of the USSR in Denmark, from 1985 to 1989 he was the Commercial Director of the firm Fershimex in Belgium, which was unusual for the Soviet years—not everyone was allowed to work abroad. In 1992, A.G. Lomakin created the International Potash Company (IPC), uniting the sales of the largest fertilizer producers—Uralkali, Sylvinit, and Belaruskali. In 1994, he became the General Director of IPC. It was at this time that Rybolovlev met O. G. Lomakin and began their partnership.

Lomakin's gang was engaged in robbery, robbery, and murder. The gangsters' arsenal of weapons included cold and firearms, including, as the investigation later pointed out, a small-caliber pistol with a silencer, several TT pistols, a Kalashnikov assault rifle, and four anti-tank grenade launchers RPG-18 "Mukha". This is what fell into the hands of the investigators. There were more weapons, and they were scattered in different locations.

Lomakin first appeared at the plant sometime in February 1995. He was introduced as Rybolovlev's "handler". Lomakin did not interfere in the activities of the plant and did not give any instructions on work at the plant to anyone—this was not his function. Lomakin's function was to get involved in all matters related to the plant, to control everything, including profits, to monitor the sale of products and the payment of dividends. Lomakin kept an eye on the money. He was not needed at the plant, and he was there not as a "curator" from Rybolovlev, but as a "curator" of the money-extorting Perm mafia.

Lomakin had his own office in the building of Neftekhimik and officially represented "the interests of the plant's shareholders" and "defended their interests." His salary was $2,000-$2,500 per month. The plant bought Lomakin a flat and gave him a new 1995 Mitsubishi Pajero SUV for his personal use. The car belonged to Neftekhimik and was leased to Lomakin under an agreement for $2.19 per month. In February 1996, Lomakin bought the car from Neftekhimik for RUB 220 million ($4,720), which was also inexpensive.

Lomakin had another dead body on his conscience. On 26 October 1995, at about 23:00 local time, Lomakin met a girl named Marina in the Grotto bar at the Ural Hotel in Perm. The next morning, he drove Marina to her home. When he was driving back, at a speed of 80-90 kilometers per hour, driving around a bus, he hit a man to death. He stopped, got out of the car, made sure that the person he had hit was dead, felt sad that he had damaged the car, and drove away. The car was indeed dented after the accident. The next day Lomakin moved the car to the area of the city university, and a few days later filed a police report that the car had been stolen while he was on a business trip (from noon on 25 October) to another city, Yekaterinburg, from which he had just returned.

On 18 March 1996, Lomakin was detained. On the same day, Kirsanov was detained. But while Kirsanov was charged with the murder of Zuev, Lomakin had only been charged so far with the murder of a pedestrian, Alexander Dunin. Lomakin pleaded not guilty. At the interrogation on 20 March, he again testified that the car was stolen from him and he did not hit the pedestrian, as he was in Yekaterinburg that day. The presence of numerous witness testimonies pointing to Lomakin as the driver of the car that hit the man did not embarrass Lomakin too much. At the next interrogation on 28 March, Lomakin again plead not guilty and confirmed his previous testimony.

And only on 2 April, at the additional interrogation, Lomakin unexpectedly stated that he had decided to change his testimony: on 27 October 1995 he had hit a man. He explained that he was changing his testimony because a man had died and he was very sad about it.

He changed his testimony because he had learned that Kirsanov had been detained, who, as Lomakin believed, would confess to Zuev's murder and point to Lomakin as the initiator of the murder. It was necessary to find some trump cards to bargain with the investigators. Lomakin found two at once: a confession of guilt in the unintentional killing of a pedestrian and a statement that Panteleimonov's murder was ordered and organized by Rybolovlev.

The description of Zuev's murder helps our research because it gives an insight into the nature of the activities of the people who were part of Lomakin's group and of Lomakin himself, one of Rybolovlev's partners.

In October 1995, Lomakin proposed to kill Zuev because he "received money to pay for the flat, but spent it all", "pocketed some of the money", "did not come in time for the murder of Panteleimonov", "did not take the gun after the murder of Panteleimonov", "used drugs" and was a "snitch". On 7 November, Lomakin's gang celebrated the anniversary of the revolution in Russia in the very flat that Zuev had not paid for, on Startseva Street. In the interrogation protocols, it was recorded: "They sat and drank alcohol, they had cognac, vodka, beer, wine. In the course of the conversation, they all decided that Zuev should be killed. It was O.G. Lomakin who expressed the need to kill Zuev. O.G. Lomakin claimed that Zuev had not paid his phone bill and that Zuev was giving away information. They jointly decided to lure Zuev out of the flat and take him out of town... O.G. Lomakin suggested killing Zuev with knives and strangling him. Everyone actively participated in the discussion. The signal for the attack was supposed to be the stopping of the car.

Lomakin himself, however, did not go anywhere but stayed in his flat on Startseva Street. Sergei Ilynykh took with him an electric wire to strangle Zuev. They stopped by Zuev's sister's house and picked up Zuev. When the car stopped, Ilynykh threw the electric wire around Zuev's neck, "tied a knot around Zuev's neck" and began to strangle him. Sergei Slabinsky started stabbing Zuev with a knife: once or twice in the head, two or three times in the stomach, wanting to "finish everything faster". Sergei Slabinsky had with him a penknife with a 7-10 cm blade (he threw it away after the murder). Vyacheslav Pachin and Igor Yu. Lomakin (namesake of O. G. Lomakin) helped pull Zuev out of the car, after which I. Yu. Lomakin and Ilynykh also began stabbing Zuev with knives. Slabinsky accidentally stabbed Ilynykh's arm twice. Zuev broke free and ran. Igor Yu. Lomakin caught up with him and finished him off with knife blows.

Ilynykh explained to the investigators that they wanted to kill Zuev quickly.

At the end of November 1995, the participants in the murder went to

Alushta to hide out, and O.G. Lomakin gave each of them $1000.

Meanwhile, Kirsanov, who had been arrested, testified that Lomakin was involved in the murder of Panteleimonov.

Lomakin was interrogated, and on 18 April 1996, he wrote a lengthy statement that Panteleimonov's murder was not actually "ordered" by him, but by Rybolovlev, and that Lomakin was only a link, but not the organizer of the murder. He claimed that Rybolovlev approached him and asked him to assist "in finding people to eliminate his rival Panteleimonov" from the position of Neftekhimik's general director. Lomakin, he said, replied that Rybolovlev "would have to pay these people himself," whereupon Rybolovlev "took the entire initiative to kill Panteleimonov himself, promising the executors $50,000, knowing that there would be two of them." Rybolovlev "handed him TT pistols in a polythene bag near the bank, then he [Oleg Lomakin] gave them to Zuev, who gave them to Yura [Kirsanov] and Sergei [Ilynykh]... Rybolovlev "should have paid them" but did not.

On 8 May, Lomakin gave additional testimony:

"In early August 1995, when O.G. Lomakin once again came to the Credit FD, which Rybolovlev headed and where Neftekhimik had an account, Rybolovlev offered him to murder Panteleimonov, promising to pay him 50,000 US dollars for it. Lomakin replied to Rybolovlev that he would first have to ask the guys he knew about it. Lomakin called Yura [Kirsanov] and Sergei [Ilynykh], residents of Alushta who were in Perm and proposed to commit the offense. He [Lomakin] met Rybolovlev and received two TT pistols from the latter. Lomakin brought these pistols to the Central Market, where he gave them to Zuev and asked him to bring the pistols to a flat on Podlesnaya Street and hand them over to Yura and Sergei. Lomakin did not personally develop the murder plan, nor did he receive any money for it. He simply passed on Rybolovlev's order to his acquaintances; if he had received money for the crime, it would have gone to Kirsanov and Ilynykh. Kirsanov and Ilynykh murdered Panteleimonov, and they kept asking when they would get the money."

In the investigative documents, it was recorded: "Lomakin is ready to confirm his testimony during face-to-face interrogation with Rybolovlev. He gave his testimony willingly, without any pressure. He repents that he "was on the same team with the people who committed these crimes". He does not complain about the conditions of detention in the cell. This part of the investigation was recorded not only in writing but also on videotape". We should add that the testimony was given in the presence of Lomakin's lawyer Alexander Ketov.

On 21 May 1996, Rybolovlev was arrested. On 22 May his deputy for the Credit FD Bank Shevtsov was arrested as well. On 23 May, Lomakin and Rybolovlev were confronted.

Rybolovlev refused to testify, citing Article 51 of the Russian Constitution, which allows him not to testify against himself. Lomakin, on the other hand, repeated that in early August 1995, when he was at Credit FD and entered Rybolovlev's office, "the latter offered him to commit the murder of Panteleimonov and find the killers. "The remuneration was agreed at $50,000," Lomakin, "asked his guys if they would agree to take on the job of hitmen, and they accepted the offer." He later agreed with Rybolovlev that Rybolovlev would hand him the pistols outside the office of Credit FD Bank. "Rybolovlev handed them over in a bag. Lomakin took the pistols and left by taxi."

"Rybolovlev told Lomakin—it was recorded in the indictment—that after Panteleimonov's murder his financial group would fully own Neftekhimik, and he would become the sole owner and receive large financial profits." Lomakin said that if "the guys accept the offer, the murder will take place." Rybolovlev planned the murder: he offered to shoot Panteleimonov with two TT pistols early in the morning when Panteleimonov left for work" and "promised $50,000 to the two hitmen."

At the interrogation on 11 June, Lomakin also testified that "Rybolovlev did not specifically explain to Lomakin the motives for eliminating Panteleimonov, and Lomakin did not ask him about it. After Panteleimonov's murder, Lomakin called Rybolovlev about the payment and flew to Moscow to see Rybolovlev, who at the time, as Lomakin remembers, was staying at the International Hotel. Lomakin traveled from the airport to see Rybolovlev and Rybolovlev told him that he could not pay at the moment and promised to pay very soon. This meeting took place in late September or early October 1995. After the New Year 1996... Rybolovlev again promised to pay $50,000... Lomakin asked to be paid in cash and dollars.

On 21 and 24 June Rybolovlev again refused to testify.

As a result, the Prosecutor's Office of the Russian Federation opened a criminal case (#4902) against the Perm organized crime group, combining several murders and the group's conspiracy to divide the privatization market of Perm.

A small linguistic digression. The Soviet and then Russian prosecutor's office, investigating the activities of people suspected of committing crimes, always called the community of these people "gang" or "criminal group", and the joint activity of these people "conspiracy" or "criminal conspiracy." People under investigation had little chance of being acquitted in court, and the investigation itself, even if you were found innocent at the end of the process, could last from nine months to two years. There was no bail system, and during the investigation, the suspect sat in prison, where conditions were always exceptionally bad and even inhumane.

The prosecutor's office indictment stated:

"In 1994 during the privatization and the auction of companies in Perm Region, D. E. Rybolovlev was the CEO of a voucher investment fund Stone Belt as well of Credit FD Bank and has entered into collusive agreement with O.G. Lomakin, V. A. Nelyubin, V. B. Chernyavsky, S. Z. Rustamov and S. E. Makarov with the intent to obtain companies' shares for the prices close to the starting bids. These companies were located in the Perm Region and were either from the chemical or oil industry: JSC Uralkali, JSC Silvinit, JSC Azot, JSC Neftekhimik, JSC Metafraks, and other companies. Furthermore, D. E. Rybolovlev sought to prevent competition from obtaining large portfolios of shares or buying the shares of these companies in the secondary market by using the colluders' influence within various criminal organizations…

By the end of 1994, a part of the agreement between Rybolovlev D.E, V. A. Shevtsov, Nelyubin, and Chernyavskiy was executed, whereby O. G. Lomakin had received a position at JSC Neftekhimik, as a representative of FD group, which was controlled by Rybolovlev… As a part of the agreement with Rybolovlev, which would lead to the division of shares, O. G. Lomakin was controlling the delivery and processing of the company's raw materials as well as their sale, which allowed him to receive unaccounted money from these transactions. This allowed Lomakin to organize a gang, arm it, and keep it on a payroll, for future acts of violence against individual civilians…

Lomakin explained that he owned 1-2% of shares in JSCB Credit FD.

He also owns 2-3% of shares in JSC Metafrax and 1% of shares in JSC Solikamskbumprom. However, he did not have any official agreements on this matter, everything was agreed verbally. There were several agreements that, if the opportunity arose, he would register shares in Neftekhimik and JSCB Credit FD in his name as an individual. All of these arrangements were made with Rybolovlev. Rybolovlev offered Chernyavsky a share in the business, to become partners. The shares purchased by Lomakin were registered in Rybolovlev's firm, as it did not make sense to keep the shareholdings in different hands. However, they did not sign anything and did not formalize any documents. In Neftekhimik, Lomakin was a representative of Credit FD Bank... and controlled the financial situation."

On 17 July 1996, S. V. Ilynykh was detained and immediately began to testify about the murders of Zuev and Panteleimonov.

If with the case of Zuev's murder, everything was clear to the investigators, the picture of the organization of Panteleimonov's murder began to look somewhat different after Ilynykh's testimony. The detainee said that the murder of Panteleimonov was organized and planned by Lomakin and that three days before Panteleimonov's murder Lomakin came to their flat in Perm at 19/1 Podlesnaya Street and told them that it was necessary to kill the General Director of Neftekhimik because he, Lomakin, "receives money from the plant and Panteleimonov wants to pay Moscow [that is to pay Rustamov], and that he had information that Panteleimonov wanted to leave him", in which case Lomakin "would no longer be at the plant". Panteleimonov at that time had already stopped giving Lomakin money, and that is why "Panteleimonov must be removed."

During interrogation on 1 August, Ilynykh explained that Lomakin received money from the plant through the sale of "unaccounted goods", but Panteleimonov wanted to get away from Lomakin under a "roof" in Moscow, about which Lomakin was informed by a call from Moscow.

As gang member Efimov testified, "The guys shot Panteleimonov because Panteleimonov began to cooperate closely with Moscow" (Rustamov) and stopped cooperating with Lomakin".

In other words, Rustamov called Lomakin and informed him that Neftekhimik would now pay tribute not to Lomakin, but to Rustamov.

Kirsanov was present at the conversation. Both volunteered to commit the murder. Lomakin described Panteleimonov to them, told them where he lived, and said that Vitaly Murakhovich would take them to Panteleimonov's house, and Zuev would wait outside. Murakhovich knew where Panteleimonov lived. Before the murder, he had visited Panteleimonov's house. Zuev was instructed to watch Panteleimonov's house and collect the necessary information: to study the location and plan of Panteleimonov's flat, "the time he left for work, the time of his return, his travel routes, the number of family members and possible escape routes after the crime." Zuev soon reported that Panteleimonov drove a jeep, indicating the time when Panteleimonov usually left for work, the floor on which Panteleimonov lived and that the building had two exits and a concierge. It was decided that the murder would take place in the morning when Panteleimonov went to work. Lomakin suggested ringing the flat doorbell and killing Panteleimonov when he came to the door.

At about 7 a.m. on 4 September 1995, Murakhovich took Ilynykh and Kirsanov in a car and dropped them off at 77b Karpinsky Street in Perm, where Panteleimonov lived. Zuev was not there. The killers waited for Panteleimonov on the landing, on the balcony, for about 15-20 minutes. Panteleimonov left the flat and called the lift. Kirsanov approached Panteleimonov and fired four shots. Panteleimonov fell down. Ilynykh, as it was then stated in the investigation materials, "approached the victim and fired one control shot in the head area from a TT pistol… The victim died at the scene of the crime." The killers left the building through the staircase opposite the main entrance. Earlier they had planned to jump from the first floor, but the door to the street turned out to be unlocked. Murakhovich was waiting for them at the agreed location. Approximately 40 minutes had elapsed since Murakhovich had brought them to Panteleimonov's house.

After killing Panteleimonov, the killers went to Murakhovich's house, changed their clothes, and left their pistols there. They lived at Zuev's flat for a week, then Murakhovich moved them to his dacha. The clothes in which they were killed were burned in the woods. Later Ilynykh learnt that Zuev had burnt the clothes. Before leaving for Alushta in the second half of September, Murakhovich brought $2000 from Lomakin to Ilynykh and Kirsanov. About a month later, Lomakin phoned them in Alushta, told them that everything was calm in Perm, and they returned to Perm. They lived at the address: 11 Startseva Street, flat 67.

On 24 July 1996 confrontations were held between Ilynykh and

Kirsanov. After Ilynykh confirmed that he and Kirsanov had killed Panteleimonov, Kirsanov stated that he would like to "talk to the investigation". Kirsanov explained that he had murdered Panteleimonov. However, at the time of the murder, he did not know that the victim was the general director of Neftekhimik. He also did not know who initiated the murder of Panteleimonov. The interrogation was recorded on video.

In July 1996, Lomakin began to refuse to give further testimony and to admit his guilt, citing Article 51 of the Constitution. And on 31 July 1996, Lomakin's lawyer Igor Avergun sent a statement from his client to the prosecutor of the Perm region, in which Lomakin indicated that he had been detained on 18 March 1996 and had previously been forced to testify that he was "involved in the murder of Panteleimonov". Lomakin now claimed that he had "perjured himself not only for himself but also for Rybolovlev, who never suggested killing Panteleimonov."

During the face-to-face interrogation of Ilynykh and Lomakin, conducted on 31 July, the day the letter to the Perm Region prosecutor was written, Lomakin stated that he "could neither refute nor confirm his previous testimony. He did not give any specific instructions to Ilynykh on the murder of Panteleimonov. He did not make any proposal to Ilynykh to kill Panteleimonov. He never gave anyone the name of the person who ordered the murder, including Ilynykh. He never promised Ilynykh a reward for the murder...He cannot corroborate his testimony. He ... never gave a weapon to anyone. Ilynykh perjures himself."

Ilynykh, for his part, insisted that it was Lomakin who suggested that he murder Panteleimonov. Lomakin assigned roles and during the conversation explained that the murder had to be committed "so that the money would not go to Moscow" (to Rustamov).

On 6 August, Lomakin told the investigation, "He will not say to what extent he will plead guilty. The only thing he wants to say is that he had no self-serving motive and was not involved in the planning of Panteleimonov's murder, as he had stated earlier in his testimony."

On 8 August, Lomakin again refused to answer the investigators' questions about whether he had made anyone "an offer to kill Panteleimonov, whether he had given anyone pistols. He explained that he had not given anyone guns and had not paid any money for the murder".

On 12 September, during the face-to-face interrogation of Kirsanov and

Lomakin, both defendants refused to testify following Article 51 of the Constitution of the Russian Federation.

On 3 October, Kirsanov refused to plead guilty and explained that he would not testify on all counts of the indictment for personal reasons. According to him, "he had previously testified differently about the murder of Panteleimonov because of the physical and psychological pressure exerted on him."

On 4 October, following Lomakin's letter to the Perm prosecutor that he had incriminated Rybolovlev, the latter agreed to testify to the investigation for the first time. Rybolovlev stated that "he did not collude with Nelyubin, Lomakin, Chernyavsky and Makarov. There was no agreement to transfer shares to these people. 15% of JSCB Credit FD was sold... to the LIPS company because of the psychological pressure that V.B. Chernyavsky exerted on Rybolovlev... He did not appoint O.G. Lomakin as the owner's representative in Neftekhimik. He knew that O.G. Lomakin was hanging around the plant, but he could not do anything about it... O.G. Lomakin represented the interests of Nelyubin, Chernyavskiy... Because of threats from Chernyavskiy, Nelyubin, Makarov, and Lomakin, he was wearing a bullet-proof vest."

Rybolovlev categorically denied the accusations of involvement in Panteleimonov's murder, emphasizing that he did not meet Lomakin to discuss the matter, did not promise to pay money for the murder, did not give Lomakin any weapons and "never ordered Panteleimonov's murder to Lomakin, because he didn't have any disagreements with Panteleimonov, he proposed Panteleimonov's candidacy for the position of the CEO. At work, they had a normal professional relationship. If there were any serious disagreements, considering the block of shares they owned, they would be able to force Panteleimonov to resign from his position without using any other methods... Therefore, he had no motives to commit this crime. Besides, from the end of 1994, V. B. Chernyavsky, V. V. Nelyubin, S. E. Makarov, and O. G. Lomakin were extorting companies' shares from Rybolovlev. Because of the difficult and unpleasant relationship with them, he would not be able to order Lomakin the assassination of Panteleimonov... When the investigation posed the question of how O. G. Lomakin got into JSC Neftekhimik, had the office there, Rybolovlev replied that it was because of the extortion... Lomakin's presence at JSC Neftekhimik also was a concession to the demand of the abovementioned individuals. These individuals gained the possibility to fully manage Rybolovlev's stock of shares and were able to influence the important decisions of the CEO."

On 7 October 1996 Kirsanov—which was another surprise for the investigation—wrote a handwritten statement in which he confessed to participation in the murder of Panteleimonov, but specified that he was persuaded to take part in the murder by Zuev (who had by then been killed) and that, According to Zuev, the "order" to kill Panteleimonov came from Chernyavsky (who died in a car crash on 25 December 1995) "Zuev told him that it was Chernyavsky who asked him to kill Panteleimonov," the investigation recorded.

Kirsanov's testimony was sent by mail by his lawyer Yaroslav Makarovsky. Lomakin and Rybolovlev, according to Kirsanov's new testimony, had nothing to do with Panteleimonov's murder.

The investigation reached a dead end. The information that Rybolovlev "ordered" Panteleimonov's murder was originally received from Lomakin. All other witnesses or suspects who said that Rybolovlev "ordered" the murder knew about it only from the words of the same Lomakin, who kept telling everyone that Rybolovlev "ordered" the murder. Rybolovlev himself was not in Perm on the day of the murder: he was in Switzerland. According to his travel documents, he was absent from Perm in those months from 28 April to 10 May, 6 August, 11 to 12 August, 26 August to 5 September, 7 September to 4 October, 6 to 23 October, and 30 October to 11 November 1995. After Panteleimonov's murder, he returned to the city for one day, on 6 September, and then left again.

Such a long absence was more likely to indicate that Rybolovlev was in hiding, fearing that he would become the next victim of the perpetrators. Indeed, on 5 October 1995 Rybolovlev wrote a statement marked "To be opened after death" stating that Nelyubin, Chernyavsky, Lomakin, and Makarov were extorting shares of Uralkali, Azot, and Neftekhimik from Rybolovlev, that Rybolovlev had been threatened since August 1995, that his kidnapping was being prepared and that there had been discussions about physically eliminating him. The statement was kept in the bank's safe.

Shortly after Panteleimonov's murder, Lomakin said in a conversation with his thugs that Rybolovlev was sabotaging him at the plant, "spreading lies about him" and that "he should be removed." At the same time,

Lomakin began to tell his subordinates that Rybolovlev had ordered the murder of Panteleimonov, promising to pay him $200,000, which he had not paid, and therefore Rybolovlev owed them $200,000. The legend about the $200,000 not paid by Rybolovlev for the murder grew with time and everyone in Lomakin's gangster organization was sure that Rybolovlev owed them either money or shares. And being in debt to gangsters was a dangerous business. Debtors were killed.

According to Oschepkov, after the murder of Panteleimonov, Rybolovlev increased his security, often hiding abroad, and once someone said to Rybolovlev on the phone: "We will find you, you can't hide from us abroad". Chernyavsky, after almost three hours of conversation with Rybolovlev, left his office and told his bodyguard P. N. Dymov that "he wanted to work normally, but they are trying to deceive him." To Shevtsov, shortly after Panteleimonov's murder, Chernyavsky said "in a rough way": "Forget about Panteleimonov. As for Rybolovlev, he's greedy, he doesn't want to share, and doesn't he realize that he could be buried?". Shevtsov immediately retold this conversation to Rybolovlev, saying that, "it has been decided to bury Rybolovlev." Nelyubin once told Rybolovlev that if he "fulfilled his obligations, he would not need a security detail of 12 guards."

Rybolovlev's relationship with the bandits was at least tense, if not hostile, by August 1995. And this most likely cleared Rybolovlev of charges that he was involved in Panteleimonov's murder. But in the course of interrogations new circumstances regarding the preparation of attempts on the bandits themselves came to light, and Rybolovlev and Shevtsov came under suspicion. To begin with, in October-November 2015, an explosive device was found under Chernyavsky's car, which, according to Chernyavsky, "was from Rybolovlev because he does not want to pay for Panteleimonov". It was set by "someone from Credit FD Bank." Chernyavsky believed that this person was Shevtsov.

Relations with Nelyubin also became hostile. From 7 August 1995, immediately after the murder of Panteleimonov, Nelyubin was no longer allowed into the Credit FD Bank without the prior consent of Rybolovlev or Shevtsov. On 29 August 1995, Nelyubin had a final falling out with Rybolovlev during their meeting and conversation in Switzerland. And in early September, Nelyubin learned that Shevtsov had ordered his murder.

Shevtsov ordered the murder of Krechetov (whom he had once asked to organize the beating of Kazantsev, the director of Neftekhimik), "explaining that he was taking out too big loans" which he was not paying back, "he had become very insolent" and "they were fed up with him". Nelyubin was to be eliminated "after 28 April". Shevtsov gave Krechetov an advance of $5,000. Another $15,000 Krechetov was to receive upon completion of the task.

However, instead of killing Nelyubin, on 18 April Krechetov exchanged $1000 and bought a TV set, and lost the rest of the money in a casino in the Izmailovo sports complex in Moscow, after which he returned to Perm and in May told Sergei Lobaev, Nelyubin's deputy, about the order.

In April and May, Nelyubin was in Cyprus. In September 1995, together with Lobaev, Krechetov flew to Moscow, where he told Nelyubin everything in person. Krechetov believed that the order came from Rybolovlev, because "Shevtsov could not have made such decisions himself". He did not ask for money for the information. But he said: "If you pay me well, I will take care of Shevtsov."

In November 1995, Nelyubin told Rustamov what had happened. Rustamov organized for Nelyubin to meet Shevtsov and Rybolovlev in Moscow. The conversation took place in the Moscow office of the bank in the presence of Rustamov and lasted 5-6 hours. It is not known what they agreed on, but Nelyubin stepped up security and began to come to Perm less often.

At the same time, the FSB Department in Perm received information about Krechetov's intention to kill Nelyubin. It seems that this information was initially received by A. V. Rychkov, an FSB officer in Perm, who summoned Shevtsov, Krechetov, and Nelyubin to talk to him. Krechetov told Rychkov that he had received an order from Shevtsov to kill Nelyubin and had received a deposit of $5000 and that Nelyubin in return offered Krechetov "under a plausible pretext to transport Shevtsov to the right bank of the Kama River and hand him over to Nelyubin's men".

On 24 September 1996, Krechetov was summoned to the Perm Department of Internal Affairs, where he spent about 20 minutes with police investigator Osipov. Osipov did not explain the reason for summoning Krechetov, but said that "there was a person who wanted to meet with him". It turned out to be one of the security officers of Credit FD, who suggested that Krechetov sign a letter addressed to the city prosecutor in which he recanted his testimony about the attack on Kazantsev and the murder of Nelyubin ordered by Shevtsov. The man said he was a representative of the bank and, if Krechetov signed a statement to that effect and had it notarized, he was "ready to pay any amount Krechetov asked for". Krechetov asked for $100,000, to which the interlocutor replied that he needed to consult with someone and scheduled a meeting for 25 September 1996 at 4 p.m. on Friendship Square in Perm. No one came to the meeting.

On 4 October 1996 Rybolovlev testified that he had not conspired with Shevtsov to plan the murder of Nelyubin and that he had "never heard the name Krechetov". Shevtsov also categorically denied all of Krechetov's accusations and said that he "does not know how the FSB learned about Krechetov, as he did not contact the FSB."

On 26 December 1995, upon his arrival in the city of Perm the day after Chernyavsky was killed in a car accident, Nelyubin was summoned to the Perm FSB. There, Nelyubin was told that they had information about Nelyubin's plans to kill Shevtsov and that Krechetov also feared an assassination attempt. Nelyubin replied that he did not plan to kill anyone, but, on the contrary, feared for his life and "has 24-hour security who escorts him at work and at home."

The FSB did not check all these facts, because Rychkov concluded that "the information about the order to kill was insignificant and the perpetrator had no intention to fulfill it."

In April 1997, after spending eleven months in prison, Rybolovlev was released. It was difficult to prosecute him: Lomakin recanted his testimony; it was impossible to prove Rybolovlev's involvement in the attempt to eliminate Chernyavsky and Nelyubin, if only because the crimes had not been committed. But in Russia, it was statistically speaking impossible to escape from the hands of the prosecutor's office after almost a year of investigation. Lomakin, Ilynykh and Kirsanov were sentenced to 15 years each. Rybolovlev was acquitted of all charges in 1998. He became the only one to be acquitted completely.

To make this happen, Rybolovlev's mother-in-law Larisa paid a bribe of $250,000 delivering money personally. The case was indeed dismissed. The negotiations to accept the bribe and to release and close the case was conducted by Rustamov, whom Rybolovlev, in his own words, "saved" and to whom he now "owed his life". Exactly how Rustamov saved Rybolovlev's life remains beyond the cardboard. But for Rybolovlev, Rustamov has since remained a friend and an authority (without inverted commas), whose opinion he always listened to.

After Panteleimonov's murder, due to squabbles among the bandits, investigations, and interrogations, Neftekhimik's sales plummeted. The company went into debt, and the share price began to fall. About 40% of the shares belonged to Rybolovlev, who sold the shares of Neftekhimik to Solvalub and used the proceeds to buy shares in Uralkali.

In October-November 1995, even before Rybolovlev and Shevtsov were arrested, Rustamov agreed with the Perm group that they would part ways with Rybolovlev and withdraw from all joint structures, businesses, and companies. "LIPS sold Rybolovlev his stake in Credit FD Bank." Rybolovlev sold his stake in LIPS to Rybolovlev. Lomakin, Chernyavsky, and Nelyubin sold shares in Neftekhimik and JSC Solikamskbumprom. In October-November 1995, the shares in JSC Uralkali and JSC Azot "due to the decision to completely stop working with Rybolovlev" were exchanged. Rybolovlev received Uralkali; the Perm group received Azot. The negotiations were conducted by Rybolovlev and Shevtsov on the one hand and Chernyavsky on the other. As a result, Rybolovlev's group and LIPS' firm divided the spheres of influence and redistributed the shares of major chemical and petrochemical enterprises in Perm and the region—Uralkali, Azot, Metafrax, Sylvinit, Neftekhimik and others. In gratitude for his services, Rustamov received from Rybolovlev the shares of Metafrax, and from the bandits what was due to him as a shareholder of LIPS.

Since August 1995, when Panteleimonov was killed, Rustamov began to spend a lot of time abroad, mainly in the US, although even in 1996 he was still registered in his flat in Perm. What he was doing between 1996 and 2000 is not quite clear. But since 2000 his biography looks flawless. According to the official version, which uses the same verbiage on several different websites, since 2000 he has been "actively involved in trading in chemical and petrochemical industry, making investments in energy funds and oil and natural gas extraction industry projects, as well as making investments in commercial and residential real estate," quickly becoming a millionaire in the process.

In August 2005, Rustamov bought a $2,45 million villa at 8410 Brookwood Court, McLean, Fairfax County, 22102 Virginia[3]. In 2011, his wife Marina Kotova (by this time they had three children) bought another mansion in Virginia for $1.6 million at 1401 Woodhurst Blvd, Mclean Virginia.

Rybolovlev's wife, according to her recollections, was very afraid of this man with "blue eyes" and "piercing gaze," but did not reveal the reasons for her fear. Not surprisingly, neither in the USA nor in Europe, Rybolovlev's connection with Rustamov was not advertised and Rustamov was not introduced to Rybolovlev's friends.

In 2014, Rustamov was a "beneficial owner of a chemical company Metafrax," which is located in the same Perm Region where Rybolovlev's business interests were concentrated. By 2017, Rustamov consolidates 92,37% of the share ownership in the company and transforms it into a group holding structure with production capacities in Russia (in Perm and Moscow Regions) and in Austria, and becomes the largest producer of methanol, formaldehyde, and synthetic resins in Russia and Europe. During that period, the annual revenue of the Metafrax Group exceeded RUB 40 million (at an average annual ruble exchange rate of RUB 58 per $1), and its distribution network includes over 50 countries worldwide.

Lomakin got out of prison early, in 2009, with a 33% stake in the West Urals Chemical Company, which was transformed into LIPS LLP. By 2009, only three partners remained there: Chernyavsky died, and Rustamov left and withdrew from LIPS. In addition, Lomakin received $960,000 in dividends that had accumulated over the years of his imprisonment. So, in the end, he got a lot more than the $200,000 he was saying he was supposed to get for Panteleimonov's murder.

But how did Rybolovlev, who got out of the pre-trial detention center in 1997 with the help of Rustamov and a $250.000 bribe, build up his business and become a multi-millionaire and then a billionaire?

Rybolovlev was not a man whose physical appearance could frighten anyone. He was not feared. He was not the head of the mafia. Nor was he a man who promoted himself at the expense of women or who got close to people during meals because he didn't drink. He was not charismatic, but he had a good understanding of how the system worked—the same one that was bribed $250,000 and got Rybolovlev out of prison. "I realized that it is extremely important to build the right relationships with many people, including the authorities. Before, I was just doing business and did not try to integrate into this system... Now I am sure that big business cannot exist outside the state," Rybolovlev said.

A delicate nuance was that the $250,000 bribe was given to the FSB, and the person who released Rybolovlev was none other than the head of the regional FSB department of the Perm region, General—eventually he became Colonel-General—Sergei Pavlovich Ezubchenko, who has become Rybolovlev's partner and handler for eternity. With the FSB's partnership and patronage, Rybolovlev (who was now "on the hook" with the State Security Service) was allowed to get on his feet, get rich and become a millionaire/billionaire. Rybolovlev could more properly be considered a manager of the Ezubchenko empire, a hired hand who carried out the instructions of the all-powerful state security general. Rybolovlev replaced his old gangster roof, which had failed to save him from an 11-month imprisonment, with the FSB roof, which, as time has shown, turned out to be exceptionally strong.

Ezubchenko was born in 1951 in Astana, the capital of Kazakhstan, into the family of a KGB officer. He graduated from high school in Ust-Kamenogorsk. In 1969 he entered the Tomsk Institute of Radio and Electrical Engineering. After graduating in 1974, he started to work for the KGB in Tomsk and Tomsk Region. From February 1993 to October 1995, he served as deputy head of the KGB Department in Chita Region. In October 1995 he was appointed to the post of the Head of the Perm Department of the FSB. In 1997 fate brought him together with Rybolovlev who was held in Perm prison. Since 1997, Ezubchenko had been acting as a high-ranking "roof" of the FSB, covering Rybolovlev, who had risen to the status of an oligarch and billionaire, with his numerous businesses in Russia and abroad.

Ezubchenko remained as head of the Perm Department of the FSB until 2002. In January 2003, the General became Deputy Director General of ZAO Permgeologodobycha, a subsidiary of Uralkali established in 2002 and engaged in exploration of diamond deposits in the Perm region. At the same time, Ezubchenko was an "assistant" (in fact, a curator from the FSB) to the Chairman of the Board of Directors of Uralkali Rybolovlev since June 2004[4].

While Rybolovlev was in prison, his fellow countryman Yuri Trutnev, born in 1956, became governor. Trutnev was a former Komsomol worker and was fond of sambo, wrestling, karate, and motor racing. In 2000, he planned to run in the election race for the position of the Governor of the Perm Region. Rybolovlev, instead of serving 15 years in prison for murder, decided to get involved in big politics and invested money in the election campaign of Perm mayor Trutnev for governor of the Perm region, where Rybolovlev had his main business. Trutnev won the first round and became governor in late 2000, and Rybolovlev, as he later recounted, "sponsored Trutnev's career," eventually rising to the position of deputy prime minister.

In flight: 2000, Trutnev's election campaign (second from left). Next to him, to his right is Rybolovlev.

In 2004, Trutnev was appointed Minister of Natural Resources and Ecology in the Russian government. This was a very lucrative post in a poor-but-natural-resources-rich country. And a very useful one: when a major accident occurred in one of the mines of Uralkali in October 2006, it was Trutnev, in his capacity as the Minister of Natural Resources and Ecology, who was heading up the government commission investigating the accident.

Rybolovlev planned to float Uralkali on the London Stock Exchange in 2006. As a result, the company significantly increased ore extraction, which in turn led to the destruction of the protective layer of mine No. 1. On 11 October 2006 (a week before the accident) Rybolovlev stopped the proposed IPO on the London Stock Exchange, possibly because he expected a disaster at the mine and decided not to risk the success of the IPO.

On 17 October 2006, the Uralkali mine in Berezniki began flooding, causing work stoppages and air pollution from underground gases. Uralkali denied that the accident was anything serious, but a few days later a 500-meter sinkhole opened up over the Berezniki mine. The scale of the disaster was significant. Newspapers dutifully called it the worst environmental disaster in the former Soviet Union since Chornobyl. Railways and energy facilities were damaged, and a significant number of residents were left homeless.

There were speculations that the mine collapsed due to the company's refusal to finance the installation of drainage pipes at the mine. A government commission was set up to investigate the causes of the accident. It was headed by Yuri Trutnev and Oleg Chirkunov, Trutnev's successor as Perm Governor. As a result of the investigation, it was determined that the combination of technological and geological factors was the cause of the accident, that the sinkholes were the result of a "previously unknown geological anomaly" and that the circumstances preceding it were extraordinary and were not the result of human error. On a personal level, Rybolovlev was absolved of responsibility for the damage caused. Thus, Rybolovlev's company got away with a small fine[5].

However, on 28 July 2007, a second sinkhole appeared 15 meters deep and covered an area of 3,500 square meters. By August 13, the sinkhole covered an area of more than 10.000 square meters, causing even more damage to homes and the city's infrastructure.

Both disasters were caused by predatory exploitation of natural resources and a lack of investment in mine safety at Uralkali's mines, which led to the flooding of part of the mine developing sinkholes under residential buildings and industrial premises in Berezniki.

At the time of the disaster, Ezubchenko was the supervisor of the security sector in the Russian presidential administration and deputy chairman of Uralkali's Board of Directors as "security adviser." Trutnev was the Minister of Natural Resources and Ecology. Everything was blamed on the earthquake.

"Trutnev saved my life," Rybolovlev was saying. "It cost me a lot, but it saved my life." He didn't even realize that it was better not to talk about such things. Corruption was a natural thing for Rybolovlev.

Since the accident led to an increase in the price of potash fertilizers in the world, Rybolovlev ended up benefiting from the accident: while in 2006 Uralkali's net profit was RUB 3,8 billion in 2007 it was already RUB 8 billion, and in 2008 it was RUB 29.4 billion. In autumn 2007 Uralkali went public. The company raised over $1 billion and ensured further growth in share prices.

But the railway in Perm Krai, damaged by the Uralkali accident, was not restored. On 29 October 2008, FSB officer Igor Sechin, First Deputy Prime Minister of the Russian Federation, hosted a meeting on the construction of a new railway in Perm Krai. Vladimir Yakunin, an FSB officer and head of Russian Railways (RZD), who was present at the meeting, stated that RZD lacked funds for the construction of the railway. Sechin supported his FSB colleague in this matter and offered Rybolovlev to pay for the construction of the railway. Rybolovlev refused. Sechin then gave the order to start a new investigation into the causes of the accident at the Uralkali mine.

The renewed investigation may have been linked to an attempt by Sechin and the Kremlin to raid Uralkali, a strategic industry privatized in the 1990s, under the pretext of an investigation. Under such a scheme, it was Igor Sechin who took Yukos from Mikhail Khodorkovsky and his shareholders (2003); Evgeny Chichvarkin's mobile phone business Euroset (2008); and, somewhat later, in 2014, Vladimir Evtushenkov's Bashkirneft (Bashkir Oil). Rybolovlev's wife recalled that during his trips to Russia in those months, her husband said that he might not return from another trip. He feared arrest or something more dramatic. In all cases, there was talk of possible confiscation of his assets.

However, all the consequences were neutralized by Rybolovlev's partners Trutnev (through the government) and Ezubchenko (through law enforcement agencies). In January 2009, Rostechnadzor announced that Uralkali must pay compensation of RUB 88,1 billion ($2,6 billion) to the state. The president of Russia at the time was Dmitry Medvedev, who briefly succeeded Putin. Trutnev spoke openly in defense of Uralkali and was supported by Medvedev, who was considered Trutnev's political patron. After numerous discussions in which Medvedev and Sechin were directly involved, with Putin acting as de facto arbiter, it was decided in March 2009 that Uralkali would pay a fine of RUB 7.8 billion ($232,8 million). A complex of man-made and geological factors was ruled as the cause of the accident[6].

Nevertheless, it was during the work of the second commission that Rybolovlev decided to sell Uralkali as soon as possible and emigrate from Russia. Sechin has become his enemy and it was too risky to continue to hold Uralkali.

Having resolved the issue of payments to the state in March 2009, Rybolovlev began negotiations with potential buyers in Russia. Rybolovlev was in preliminary talks on the sale of a controlling stake in Uralkali with Vladimir Lisin, owner of Novolipetsk Steel; Vladimir Potanin, owner of Norilsk Nickel; Mikhail Prokhorov and Suleiman Kerimov, co-owners of Polyus Gold. Rybolovlev himself had gained full control of Uralkali in 2000, consolidating more than 50% of its shares. In May 2010, when he sold the company, he owned about 65,5% of the shares.

On 14 June 2010, Rybolovlev, through his company Madura Holding Ltd. sold a 53,2% stake in Uralkali to Suleiman Kerimov (38,2%) and Alexander Nesis (15%) for $5,32 billion. Rybolovlev also had a stake in the potash company Sylvinit, which was also sold after Uralkali announced its intention to buy the company in December 2010. On 16 June 2011, Uralkali merged with Sylvinit. Rybolovlev was believed to have made more than $6,5 billion from these sales. His total fortune was estimated at around $9 billion. He was the 14th richest man in Russia. However, Rybolovlev's wife believed that one-third of his fortune belonged to Trutnev. Trutnev had a large family to feed by 2006: a third wife and five children. We can only assume that the second third of the capital belonged to Ezubchenko who also had a family, but this story will be addressed below.

2

If At First You Don't Succeed, Try, Try Again

Donald Trump in Search of Russian Money
and the Story of a Photograph

Mikhail Babel had never planned to become famous. He just wanted to become rich. And all others in this photo taken in gloomy Moscow in 2007 unlikely had anything but money on their minds. Here is the photo. It shows the people who are now recognizable by many worldwide.

To be precise, all but one person in this picture is recognizable by many. Meanwhile, he is the most important character in the picture. For the sake of completeness, here is the cast of characters (from left to right): Elena Baronova (after immigrating to the US, she started spelling her last name in a foreign manner: Baronoff), a real estate broker for Trump in Florida; Ivanka Trump, the daughter of Donald Trump; Michael Dezer, CEO of Dezer Development, the exclusive Trump's developer in Florida; Mikhail Babel, who will be described below; Donald Trump Jr. and Eric Trump, the sons of Donald Trump. In the Trump Organization, Donald Trump Jr. supervised construction projects. (Jared Kushner, who married Ivanka Trump on October 25, 2009, was not yet a part of the Trump family at the time this photo was taken.)

It was to drum up business that brought these Americans to gloomy Moscow at the time. However, Donald Trump himself was a frequent guest in the USSR and had formed a very favorable impressions from his trips to Russia. His July 1987 journey, for example, he described as "an extraordinary experience" and mentioned that he stayed in the "Lenin suite" at the National Hotel[7] (many years later, in 2013, Trump would stay in the "Obama suite" at the Ritz-Carlton Hotel).

In 1987 Trump was negotiating with Goskominturist (the State Foreign Tourism Committee in the USSR) regarding the construction of a luxury hotel at the center of Moscow. Local media even announced that Trump had agreed to refurbish the Soviet-era Hotel Moscow; however, the project never materialized.

In December 1996, the Moscow government officials were negotiating with Trump regarding the reconstruction and renovation of the two hotels—Hotel Moscow and Hotel Russia, with an estimated cost of about $300 million. However, as was the case previously, the parties failed to reach an agreement. The Russian media reported in 1998 that Trump was willing to invest about $200 million into the reconstruction of Hotel Moscow in exchange for being a 65-percent stakeholder in the project. In addition, around the same time, Trump considered building a skyscraper in Moscow but the project never took off as Moscow Deputy Mayor Vladimir Resin did not approve of the issuance of the construction permit, stating, "We will not build any skyscrapers in a historic part of the city as we have no right to turn a historic area into Manhattan." This must have been about the proposal to erect a 51-58-floor building on Novy Arbat Street at the center of Moscow.

The negotiations were renewed in 2004 but instead of new construction and renovation, Trump was now interested in franchising, which involved exclusively the monetizing of his name. The co-owner of MosCityGroup, Pavel Fuks, was keenly interested in Trump's brand at the time. "I had an idea to use Trump's name for one of the towers that were under construction in Moscow City—i.e., 'Imperia Tower'. However, no agreement was reached," Pavel Fuks said in an interview for the Russian newspaper *Kommersant*[8].

The issue was that Trump was not willing to invest anything upfront but wanted to receive a 20-25% stake in the project for the right to use his name and brand. As an overall investment in the Imperia Tower project was estimated at approximately $1.2 billion, Fuchs would have had to pay Trump $240-$300 million in the form of a franchising fee, which was deemed by him to be too steep.

The Trumps needed Russian money at the time because of their financial difficulties. In 2004, Trump filed for bankruptcy for the Trump Hotels and Casino Resorts, which affected three casinos in Atlantic City and one in Indiana. The bankruptcy allowed Trump to get out of an estimated $1.8 billion in debt. In 2006 he had to pledge the Trump SoHo Luxury Hotel. In connection to this, he was investigated by the Federal Government since it was alleged that much of the money that financed the development in Manhattan came from a shadowy Iceland-based corporate entity, which has been "mostly Russian."[9]

In November of 2007, Trump arrived in Moscow as a guest of the Moscow Millionaire Fair that opened on November 22, 2007, at the Crocus Expo Center. He was promoting Trump Vodka, for $40-50 per bottle. The spirit was produced by Drinks Americas Holdings, a US-based company. However, the sales of Trump Vodka failed to get proper traction in Russia and its production was stopped in 2009. Stanislav Kaufman, a brand manager at Vinexim (a company that produces vodka "Putinka"), stated that "Donald Trump's name has zero relation to vodka" while in Russia, vodka consumption is not based on image or status, but instead involves a whole range of philosophies which cannot be understood by an American manufacturer"[10].

Still, at the Millionaire Fair, Trump met one "useful" Russian-American—a Belarus-born Siarhei Kukuts, more commonly known as Sergei Millian[11]. Right away, Trump invited Millian to a horse race in Miami.

Millian graduated from the Minsk State Linguistic University in 2000. He never mentioned the circumstances of his arrival in the US. In 2006, he founded the Russian-American Chamber of Commerce (RACC) and a translation bureau in Atlanta; after that, he became a real estate broker specializing in residential and commercial real estate in the US and abroad.

Millian supported closer commercial ties between Russia and the United States, assisting US companies looking to conduct business in Russia. In 2009, RACC appealed to the US Congress "to foster necessary political changes to produce a healthier economic environment" and to grant permanent normal trade relations status to Russia. Its website noted that it "facilitates cooperation for U.S. members with the Russian Government, Russian Regional Administrations, U.S. Consulates in Russia, Chambers of Commerce in Russia, and corporate leaders from CIS [Commonwealth of Independent States] countries."

Millian also assisted Trump in "studying the Moscow market" for potential real estate investments. "Later," Millian said, "we met at his office in New York, where he introduced me to his right-hand man—Michael Cohen… All contracts go through him. Subsequently, a contract was signed with me to promote one of their real estate projects in Russia and the CIS. You can say I was their exclusive broker."

Millian was working with Russian investors looking to buy property in the United States. "We have signed formal agreements with Richard Bowers and Co., the Trump Organization, and The Related Group", he said, "to jointly service the Russian clients' commercial, residential, and industrial real estate needs… In general, Trump has a very positive attitude towards Russians because he sees them as clients for his businesses. Incidentally, he has done many projects with people from the Russian-language diaspora—for example, the development of Trump SoHo in New York with billionaire Tamir Sapir", a real estate developer from the former Soviet republic of Georgia.

The last time Millian and Trump spoke was in 2008[12], but it was Millian who became one of the sources providing information that formed a basis for the so-called Trump Dossier that triggered an ongoing investigation of the alleged Trump-Russia connection and the compromising material on Trump allegedly in the possession of the Kremlin and the FSB[13].

In 2007-2008 Trump was discussing business with yet another person of questionable background: Shalva Chigirinsky, the owner of Russian Land Ltd. This Georgian-born businessman was one of the richest men in Russia at the time. He made the list of the wealthiest Russians compiled by the Institute for the Study of the Reform for the first time in 1995, coming in 15th place. According to Forbes, as of 2007, Chigirinsky's fortune was estimated at $1,6 billion. In 2008, he was ranked by Forbes as the 524th wealthiest entrepreneur in the world, with an estimated net worth of $2.3 billion.

Shalva Chigirinsky was born in 1949, in Kutaisi, Soviet Georgia. After graduating from First Moscow State Medical Institute, Chigirinsky became an antiques dealer. In 1987, he moved to Spain and later to Germany where he lived for three years while working as a realtor. In 1989, Chigirinsky and a German businessman Ivot Shtok together founded a development company, S&T Group, which specialized in real estate developments in Moscow, with Chigirinsky becoming the Chairman of the Board of Directors of that entity in 1997. In December of 2004, S&T Development, one of the entities within S&T Group, won a tender to become an investor in the demolition of the Hotel Rossia in Moscow and subsequent development of the area in the center of Moscow called Zaryadye. Later yet, in 2007, Chigirinsky transferred the ownership of all of his development projects to Russian Land Ltd.

In the 1990s, while running his real estate development business, Chigirinsky became interested in the oil business. In 1996, jointly with British Petroleum, he founded Petrolcomplex Company for the development of a network of gas stations in Moscow. In 1999, Chigirinsky joined the Board of Directors of Sibir Energy, a British company focused on oil exploration, extraction, and refinery. In 2000, he launched and became the president of Moscow Oil Company MNK. In January 2001, he also became the president of Central Fuel Company, the principal owner of Moscow Oil Refinement Factory MNPSZ. Furthermore, in 2003, Chigirinsky became the general director, and in 2004, the president of Moscow Oil and Gas Company MNGK, where the then-mayor of Moscow, Yury Luzhkov, was the Chairman of the Board of Directors. In 2010, Chigirinsky transferred his 23.3% share ownership in Sibir Energy to Gazprom-Neft.

Among his other possessions, Chigirinsky could boast a villa on the French Riviera (Côte d'Azur) that previously had been owned by Zaire's military dictator Mobutu; Hugh House mansion in London; villa Maria Irina in France; Hotel Sovetskaya on Leningradsky Avenue in Moscow; apartments on Romanov Lane and Maly Patriarchy Lane in Moscow; as well as a collection of some 50 Fabergé watches.

By the time of Chigirinsky and Trump's meeting, Chigirinsky's track record included projects by Russian Land Ltd. involving the demolition of Hotel Rossiya, plans for the construction of Rossiya Tower in Moscow City, and many others.

However, the Chigirinsky-Trump negotiations led nowhere. In 2008, amid the global real estate crisis, Chigirinsky's business suffered a series of setbacks. Many of his large projects in Moscow had to be abandoned, including his construction of Rossiya Tower and his stake in the Crystal Island project. November 2008 saw the suspension of the construction of an ambitious 118-floor, 612-meter (2000 feet)-high building that was intended to become the highest building in Europe and to accommodate approximately 25,000 people. When Chigirinsky commenced this project in 2007, its cost was estimated at approximately $2 billion.

In early April 2009, Sibir Energy announced that it filed a lawsuit against Chigirinsky in the High Court of Justice of England and Wales (EWHC), seeking $325 million in compensation. In July 2009 Chigirinsky faced several other legal predicaments. After Vneshtorgbank's loan of RUB 3 billion to Russian Land Ltd. personally guaranteed by Chigirinsky became overdue, EWHC froze Chigirinsky's assets, including his business assets, real estate, and even his antique watch collection. In addition, in July 2009, the Central Investigation Department—Internal Affairs (Moscow) accused his companies MNK and MNGK of tax evasion to the magnitude of approximately RUB 600 million dating back to the very time that Chigirinsky was the president of both companies.

In August 2010, Chigirinsky lost the last one of his big development projects in Russia, Hotel Sovetskaya. Eventually, two criminal lawsuits were commenced against Chigirinsky on account of the alleged tax evasion. By that time, his creditors were after his properties outside of Russia. In particular, as part of the $400 million lawsuit against him, he lost Marina Irina villa on Cap Martin and his Hugh House in London. By 2009, his fortune has shrunk to a "mere" $600 million. The number of lawsuits commenced against Chigirinsky, as well as the number of lawsuits commenced by Chigirinsky himself, in different parts of the world, cannot be cataloged easily.

As it was getting tougher and tougher for him to remain in Russia, Chigirinsky was forced to flee in March 2009—first to England where he applied for political asylum, subsequently to Israel where he obtained Israeli citizenship, and eventually to the US where he settled in a rich town of Greenwich, Connecticut.

While still in Russia, Chigirinsky divorced Tatyana Panchenkova who was also residing in Greenwich. In November of 2012, Panchenkova accused her ex-husband of various forms of mental and physical abuse, which allegedly lasted for the entire duration of their more than 10 years of marriage; she even accused him of sexually abusing their daughter. Panchenkova demanded $2 million in compensation for these transgressions. Chigirinsky was arrested in March 2016 but released on a $50,000 bail. He was under investigation for 11 months and, in early February 2017, soon after Trump's inauguration, the Superior Court of Connecticut dismissed all the charges of family violence against Chigirinsky. Yet, as soon as on February 21, 2017, he was subpoenaed by the Grand Jury on account of alleged financial and tax violations in the US and was ordered to produce all relevant financial documentation.

But let's get back to that original photo from 2007. In freezing Moscow, Ivanka Trump and Elena Baronoff received as gifts fur coats made of the most expensive animal on the market—ermine. After that, the negotiations began, of which very little is known. They were led by Mikhail Babel, a participant in the collective photography.

Babel was born in 1962. In 1984, he graduated from Moscow Construction Engineering Institute as a construction engineer, and for the next 30 years, worked in the construction business in Moscow, its suburbs, and in other Russian regions. In 2003, he was promoted to the First Deputy Chairman and then to the Vice-President of the major Moscow construction company Glavmosstroy. He became the president of Glavmosstroy in 2006.

Somewhat earlier, in 1994, Babel set up NBM-Stroyservice, a construction company, which he used in 2006 as a foundation for establishing NBM, a development group, through which he became an exclusive developer for a Soviet-time KGB spy Shabtai Kalmanovich, who received a 9-year prison sentence in Israel in 1988 for espionage for the USSR. Kalmanovich was released from prison in March 1993 after numerous petitions from the Russian Government.

After his return to Russia, Kalmanovich became a successful business-man, which included being one of the leaders of an organized crime group called Solntsevo, a producer for Russian rock star Zemfira, and an owner of several basketball teams in Russia and Lithuania (including a female basket-ball team *Spartak*). In addition, Kalmanovich remained one of the most powerful players in the Russian pharmacology market, as well as a personal friend of organized crime boss, Vyacheslav Ivankov (a/k/a "Yaponchik") and another suspected crime boss, Semion Mogilevich. Babel was in charge of construction projects for Kalmanovich's organization. In particular, he was in charge of building a home office for Kalmanovich's umbrella enter-prise on Makeev Street and developing an infrastructure for the female bas-ketball team *Spartak* in the town of Vidnoe in Moscow suburbs (he even obtained a new registered office for his own company in that town).

During the 2000s, NBM developed several residential complexes in Podolsk and Krasnogorsk and started to venture into the banking business. By 2008, NBM subsidiaries could be found among shareholders of the Bank Peresvet holding about 25% of its shares.

In the following years, Bank Peresvet actively sponsored its sharehold-ers' projects. Among others, it financed the construction of residential developments. The developer promised that construction would be finished «in 18-24 months» but the project was never completed. In 2007, just one of the five of the residential construction components was ready (while the list of investors consisted of as many as 1,200 individuals).

On many projects NBM partnered with the Rose Group (RGI) on many projects, including, for example, a construction project called "In the Forest" for erecting 1.6 million square meters of residential properties in Otradnoe, Krasnogorsk district. RGI was also planning on building the Chelsea apartment building spanning about 263,000 square meters of living space. In July 2007, RGI reported to its investors that its assets had a fair market value of more than $190 million. Mikhail Babel not only received his share of the assets but also retained an approximately 27% stake of "In the

Forest" project.[14] Notably, all these shenanigans were carried out under the auspices of Kalmanovich, a legendary KGB/FSB spy.

Babel's partnership with Kalmanovich ended abruptly on November 2, 2009, when the latter was assassinated in broad daylight in the center of Moscow and died on the spot after his Mercedes was shelled by two unknown gunmen with automatic firearms. Kalmanovich's driver, Petr Tumanov, was gravely injured. Inside the car, the investigators discovered $1.5 million in cash that somehow remained untouched by the attackers.

In order not to put all of the eggs in one basket, Babel joined Glavmosstroy as its vice president in 2003. Glavmosstroy was an integral part of the Glavstroy Group owned by Basic Element, Oleg Deripaska's industrial group. It seems that its business partnership with Babel was also along the lines of collaboration with Russian intelligence agencies. According to Iskander Muhamudov, Deripaska's business partner, Deripaska was an FSB agent at least since the late 1990s, after having given his written consent to work for the FSB. Such consent was obtained by coercion from the Russian government and the FSB, threatening to take away his business. Notably, Iskander Muhamudov himself had given similar written consent. Deripaska would later become a Kremlin/FSB handler of Paul Manafort, a future Trump's Presidential Campaign manager. Manafort also became the adviser for USA-related activity for Rybolovlev.

As part of his association with Deripaska's Glavmosstroy, Babel (who, may we suppose, being a business associate of Kalmanovich and Deripaska, was an FSB agent in his own right?) happened (or was ordered) to invite to Moscow a group, which included Donald Trump, his children, his developer Dezer and a real estate broker Baronoff, who accompanied Dezer on all of his trips.

Baronoff's biography also seems to raise many questions. In 1989, she emigrated from the USSR, finding herself in Iowa and subsequently relocating to, and settling in, Florida, where she first became a travel agent and eventually a real estate broker. By 2004, she was listed as a Vice President of Customer Relations, at Trump Grande, one of the subsidiaries in the Trump Organization's corporate group. She was featured alongside Trump and his daughter Ivanka on *The Women's City* magazine cover, with the article branding her as "Donald Trump's Russian Hand."[15] At the same time, without going into any details, she notes in her biography that she was "serving as a cultural attaché in public diplomatic branches of the Russian Government." It is not clear what exactly she meant by it and whether she worked for the Russian Government. Anecdotally, cultural attaché positions in Russian embassies were well known as a cover-up for the KGB/FSB officers. Hence, Baronoff's murky autobiographical details led some reporters to speculate that she was a Soviet secret service officer and a Soviet/Russian spy in the United States[16].

Baronoff's professional activities as a real estate broker in the Trump Organization did not diminish any suspicions of her potential role as a spy because, unfortunately for her, a notorious Russian "sleeper spy" Anna Chapman also happened to have been using a cover of a real estate broker in the US at the time she was discovered and deported to Russia in a spy swap deal. Baronoff's latest title obtained in 2008—namely, the International Ambassador of the City of Sunny Isles Beach (the same city in Florida where Trump was selling residences developed by Michael Dezer to the Russian clients through Baronoff)—only confirmed the suspicions that, after visiting Moscow, the Trump Organization developed a scheme to sell properties to the Russians. The sales were soaring. This is how the Dezer Development website describes its business:

"Dezer Development was founded in 1970 by creative and innovative real estate visionary, Michael Dezer. With the involvement of his son, Gil Dezer, President of Dezer Development, the company has grown to encompass unique and strategic holdings in New York, Florida, and Las Vegas over the past 45 years. In 1985, the Dezers began to acquire ocean-front hotel properties in South Florida. Today, with just over 27 oceanfront acres, Dezer Development has arguably one of the largest holdings of beachfront property owned and developable in the state. Most of this prop-erty is earmarked for redevelopment as mid- and high-rise luxury condo-miniums, hotels, resorts, and rental communities. The renowned father and son team are credited as major players in the rebirth of Sunny Isles Beach, having developed nine luxury high-rise residential and condo-hotel[s]. Dezer Development's branded real estate portfolio includes six Trump-branded towers, a Porsche Design Tower, and Residences by Armani Casa. Generating an unprecedented response from a broad range of local, nation-al, and international buyers, the prolific developer has successfully sold over 2,700 units and generated over $3.6 billion in sales. In addition to their

Miami Beach properties, the Dezers have significant holdings in New York. Their portfolio encompasses more than 20 properties with over one million square feet."

No special gimmicks were necessary for the scheme to be successful. It is just that neither the Trump Organization members nor Baronoff's firm asked any questions about the origins of the buyers' money. Any Russian official or law enforcement officer, however corrupt, and any kind of Russian businessman, whether law-abiding or not, regardless of the source of his/her wealth, was welcome to purchase real estate in Trump's elite developments. All that they had to do was wire the requisite funds to the seller, whether from a personal, corporate, offshore, Russian, or non-Russian account, whether it was an account in their name or the name of someone else. There were cases when senior executives of corporations or banks used corporate funds to purchase properties for themselves, without the knowledge or approval of the Board of Directors or shareholders. And in the instances where such a blatant and straightforward way of conducting business was for some reason not desirable, an additional "buffer" in the form of a US-based attorney would be involved, whereby a payment from the buyer would first be transferred to an attorney, who, in turn, would transfer the requisite funds on behalf of his/her client to the seller (either an entity at the Trump Organization or an intermediary selling apartment in one of Trump's buildings).

If a Russian buyer could not finance his/her entire purchase with cash but could advance a down payment of 50% or more of the purchase price, Baronoff arranged for financing through her channels. The lenders in such cases were often recommended by Baronoff's son George Baronoff, also a real estate broker in Florida.

The foregoing seems to be the key to Trump's success in dealing with clients from countries with underdeveloped market economies, be it Trump Tower in Panama or Miami. One of the sources estimates that in five of Trump buildings in Miami, clients from the former Soviet Union/Russia made up about 50% of the population (notably, in the three smaller towns near Miami—Sunny Isles, Hallandale, and Hollywood—there were approximately 30,000 «Russians»). For similar reasons, Trump's sixth skyscraper was mostly occupied by Hispanics of Latin/South American origin.

In modern reality, failure to verify the sources of funds in a real estate deal renders both parties responsible for a potential money laundering scheme. However, to clarify the answers to all of the open questions with Elena Baronoff herself is impossible. In 2014 she was diagnosed with leukemia and died the following year. Elena's son, George Baronoff, was then firmly established as a Florida real estate broker for the Trump Organization.

Still, here is a brief narrative provided at my request by another Florida real estate broker regarding Trump/Dezer skyscraper developments: "We estimate that there have to be at least 300 tenants/apartment owners in each building, with at least half comprised of the "Russians". I'd say that the cheapest unit costs about $1,1 million—and this is for all of the five buildings plus the new Porsche Building" (that has no Trump name).

Naturally, Dezer needed seed money to start any skyscraper construction. This funding was provided by the banks. It is useful to describe here the history of the relationship between the Trump/Trump Organization and the German Deutsche Bank.

Since 1998, Deutsche Bank extended $2.5 billion in loans to Trump's companies, including $125 million that were advanced for the reconstruction of a New York skyscraper. In 2005, Deutsche Bank lent Trump $640 million for the construction of a high-rise building in Chicago. The applicable charges that Deutsche Bank was entitled to receive in this deal were approximately $12.5 million but, due to the mortgage and financial crises of 2008, Trump underpaid Deutsche Bank about $40 million on the basis that the crisis ought to be considered force majeure and thus should excuse the underpayment. Bank attempted to collect the shortage through legal means but Trump counterclaimed, seeking compensation for the $3 billion loss incurred by his organization on the basis that the Bank was responsible for the financial crisis, which led to the loss.

While the court did not buy Trump's arguments, it ordered Deutsche Bank to restructure the relevant debt. The term of the borrowing was extended and, in 2012, it was finally settled on new conditions. After that, Trump turned into a persona non-grata for the credit department at Deutsche Bank. Similarly, Citibank, JP Morgan Chase, and Morgan Stanley do not do business with Trump on account of his several bankruptcies. The Goldman Sachs executives also "have enough sanity to keep away from any deals related to Trump"[17] according to one of the bank's former top managers quoted in Wall Street Journal. But for the private banking division of Deutsche Bank, Trump remains a valued client. Just during the 2012-2015 period, this division financed $170 million of Trump's Washington hotel construction and $125 million of his development projects in Miami.

To be fair, neither the bank nor the Trump Organization disclosed the exact terms and amounts of the borrowings, and thus these figures may not be entirely accurate. There were even rumors that the loans extended to Trump by Deutsche Bank were issued by Vnesheconombank, a Russian Government-owned financial institution, through the Bank of Cyprus as an intermediary. To that end, a meeting between Trump's son-in-law, Jared Kushner, and Sergei Gorkov, an FSB officer and the Chairman of Vnesheconombank, which took place in Washington in December 2016, soon after Trump was elected as the President of the US, was about the financial situation of Trump Organization, including the situation with the old and new borrowings.

Deutsche Bank's Russia branch merits particular attention. On May 12, 2006, the Bank announced that Ilya Sherbovich and Nicholas Jordan were appointed as managers of the Branch. In particular, the announcement stated that Sherbovich had been employed by the Bank for over 10 years and participated in many transactions to which Deutsche Bank's Russia branch was a party:

Advising Gazprom on the sale of its 10.74% stake to Rosneftegaz and its $13 billion acquisition of Sibneft; arranging for a buyer consortium to acquire a 34.5% ownership stake in Magnitogorsk Iron & Steel Works factory... through privatization and direct purchase; advising the Russian Federal Property Fund in connection with the privatization of a 7.59% ownership stake in Lukoil; advising a major juice producer Multon on the sale of its assets to Coca-Cola. Sherbovich is also credited with establishing one of Russia's most advanced teams in the Russian stock market, which participated in several initial public offerings at both Russian and non-Russian stock exchanges of the major Russian companies, including the telecommunications company Comstar-OTS, Russia's largest consumer-oriented private sector company AFK Sistema, the supermarket giant The Seventh Continent and the juice producing enterprise Lebedyansky.

Jordan has been with Deutsche Bank since 1996. A graduate of Boston University, he spent 10 years at Chemical Bank in New York before transferring to Deutsche Morgan Grenfell to manage its operations in Russia in 1997-1999. During that time, Morgan Grenfell Securities was considered one of Russia's top five equity brokerage houses and was a leader in the local currency and financial market which helped to advance Russian companies to the international capital markets and advise clients on some of Russia's largest M&A transactions. "Ilya and Nicholas have reputations as leading investment bankers in the Russian market. They will become a major resource as we continue to develop investment banking services and strengthen our presence in the market," said in this context Charles Ryan, a Regional Leader and Chief Executive Officer of the Deutsche Bank Group in Russia.

Since at least 2005, another Russian-born individual in the US became Trump's agent in Russia. The individual in question is Felix Sater, a man of dubious reputation, with convictions for a first-degree assault and fraud in the US, with alleged Russian mafia connection, and with childhood and business connection to Trump's lawyer, Michael Cohen. Sater's name is consistently mentioned alongside Cohen's, as well as in the context of the Trump Organization's projects—which explains why he would become one of the main persons of interest in the Mueller investigation.

In 2005, Felix Sater was pursuing an ambitious plan in Moscow to build a Trump Tower on the site of an old pencil factory along the Moscow River bank that would offer hotel rooms, condominiums, and commercial office space. Letters of intent had been signed and square footage was being analyzed. "There was an opportunity to explore building Trump Towers internationally," said Mr. Sater, who worked for a New York-based development company that was a partner with Donald Trump on a variety of deals during that decade, "and Russia was one of the countries" where Trump Towers could be built.

In 2006, Sater traveled to Moscow again with two of Trump's children, Donald Jr. and Ivanka, who stayed in the Hotel National for several days to see promising partners, with the intent of striking real estate development deals. "Let's do a deal here," Sater stated and "arranged for Ivanka to sit in Putin's private chair at his desk and office in the Kremlin."[18]

It was through Sater that Trump also met Tevfik Arif, formerly a Soviet government official from Kazakhstan and founder of a development company called the Bayrock Group, of which Sater was also a partner. Bayrock was also interested in deals in Russia. As described by Sater himself, "We looked at some very, very large properties in Russia," "think of a large Vegas high-rise."[19]

In 2007, Bayrock brokered a potential deal in Moscow between Trump International Hotel and Russian investors. The Trump Organization representatives discussed a plan to construct in Moscow a 58-floor analog of New York's Trump Tower and hoped to sell the right to use the brand name. In April 2007, the Trump trademark was registered in connection with the provision of services in residential, commercial, and hospitality real estate.

In 2008, the Trumps were most interested in building hotels utilizing an approach similar to that employed in building condominiums under the "Trump International Hotel & Tower" brand. "Moscow is the perfect market, and it is exactly the place where we should be," stated Donald Trump Jr. He emphasized that, unlike in New York, there was still a lot of space in Moscow to realize large-scale real estate developments. "We want to enter the Russian market with a meaningful project,"—he said, adding, without naming any names, that the Trumps had had meetings with several Russian real estate developers. "As no agreements have been reached yet, it is too early to talk specifics," he said.

But, as in 2004, Trump had no intention of building anything in Russia and investing in Russia. Maksim Temnikov, a member of the Board of Directors of the Mirax Group, mentioned in this regard that Trump was only willing to work in Russia as a franchisor but that the franchising business model was not attractive to his potential business partners: "Our market is already mature and major companies would not be interested in this type of business venture. Alexei Belousov, a commercial director at the Capital Group shared that view: "Russian real estate market is at another level of development, and the time of franchising is gone", but many people might be interested in American corporate experience and investments[20].

Russian developers were wary of dealing with Trump. "There is no guarantee that in Russia the Trump brand would enjoy the same success as in America where people were willing to pay extra 20-30% for the Trump-branded properties," offered Maksim Temnikov. That view was shared by

Alexey Belousov: "For Russian companies, the value of this brand is not obvious." Turkhan Makhmudov, a Managing Director at BBDO Branding, also noted that the Trump brand was not widely recognized in Russia.

However, the popularity of the Trump brand was declining even in the US. If the brand was ranked seventh in 2004, yielding in popularity only such brand names as Apple, Google, Target, Starbucks, Pixar, and Amazon.com, it moved down to 24th place in 2005, and to 48th place in 2006. Such was the backdrop against which to view Trump's efforts to enter the Russian real estate market with his brand since Russian funds appeared to be the only reliable source of capital.

3

Saving Donald Trump

The year 2008 turned out to be no less fateful for Trump than the year 2000. The financial crisis that hit the US affected the property market; Trump's empire was (not for the first time, but for the sixth time) on the verge of bankruptcy, which meant the end of Trump as a businessman and politician. Only Russian money could save the situation. Rybolovlev came to the rescue. He paid Donald Trump for the villa, which at 2008 prices cost... It wasn't worth anything, that villa. Trump bought it at auction for about $41.35 million in 2004. It looks like he put some money into renovations: remodeling the interior of the main house, installing new kitchens, and dividing the great room to create additional bedrooms and bathrooms, as well as making minor changes to doors, frames, and windows. This is according to the documents. "I tidied it up a little bit, but not too much. The main thing is I painted it,—Trump talked about the renovations in an interview.

In July 2006, he put it up for sale for $125 million but failed to sell it. In March 2008, he lowered the price to $100 million. But in 2008, when property prices collapsed due to the global economic crisis, it was impossible to sell it.

In May 2008, Rybolovlev decided to rescue Donald Trump from his sixth bankruptcy and pay him $95 million for a villa that, according to the then-prevalent pricing was worth probably nothing. Trump purchased said villa for approximately $41.4 million in 2004. He may or may not have made some capital repairs since then. He listed it for sale in 2006 but was unable to sell it. By 2008, given the downfall of the real estate prices, it was impossible to sell. The villa stood uninhabited and growing mold. All of a sudden, Trump "lucked out" since some "crazy Russian" bought it for $95 million.

A "crazy Russian" turned out to be Rybolovlev. According to the testimony of Rybolovlev's ex-wife, Elena Chuprakova, on 1-2 April 2006, Rybolovlev, Elena, and their Russian-American friends Rustamov (who "saved" him in 1996-1997) and his wife Marina Kotova, found themselves near the villa in question and were able to see the property from the outside, entering the lot from the beach. Two years later (during which time no one expressed any interest in the villa, except Florida mold—which speaks volumes regarding the reasonableness of the ultimate selling price), on 3-6 May 2008, Rybolovlev found himself in Florida again without his wife, and, this time, decided to buy the villa.

From the somewhat confusing, as far as the purchase of Trump's villa is concerned, the testimony of Elena Rybolovleva, under oath in a Swiss court, it appears that Rybolovlev planned to make this purchase without consulting his wife. "Immediately after visiting the property, Dmitri told me that he had directed [his employee] Serguei Vakula to start the purchase negotiations with Mr. Trump's representatives, which negotiations were finalized by Mr. Mikhail Sazonov," Rybolovleva testified in court. This testimony showed that Rybolovlev did not consult his wife on the purchase of the villa. Dmitry organized its purchase "behind my back,"—Elena told the court under oath. The money to buy the villa came from accounts outside of his wife's control:

"Little did I know at the time that Dmitri was already arranging to purchase the property, using assets acquired during our marriage in a manner such that it would be unavailable to me. namely through a limited liability company and a trust. I have since learned that Dmitri was represented by Carol Digges of Brown Harris Stevens Residential Sales... Ms. Digges has reported that Dmitri visited the property with a friend who spoke more fluent English than Dmitri (presumably Serguei Vakula) who could only say "hello" in English. Ms. Digges further reported that they walked through the house for about an hour and had very little conversation. After the tour, Dmitri expressed an interest in purchasing the property. Lawrence Moens, of Lawrence A. Moens Associates, Inc., 245 Sunrise Avenue, Palm Beach, Florida, represented Donald Trump. Again, as reported, Lawrence Moens had with him a contract that had been approved by his client Donald Trump.

Dmitri signed the contract at the property and then left. Dmitri was represented by Robert Brody, Esq. in connection with the closing of the transaction."

In other words, by 3-6 May everything had already been discussed and agreed upon in connection with the upcoming purchase of Trump's villa: papers were prepared, brokers and lawyers were assembled...

Rybolovlev informed his wife that the villa, which Elena never saw, had been purchased only after the deal had been completed "on or about 5 May 2008" Rybolovleva reports uncertainly. It is clear why: the County Road Property LLC, the company under which the villa was to be purchased, was registered on 9 May in secret from his wife. On 12 May, a trust was set up in the name of wife Elena and daughter Anna, which paid for the villa. But the wife was also unaware of the trust. The transaction was executed by Mikhail Sazonov, Rybolovlev's trustee. Rybolovlev himself, after having instructed to buy the villa, had nothing more to do with it.

Rybolovlev would never have allowed himself to buy Trump's villa without coordinating the purchase with his Russian partners Trutnev and Ezubchenko, and given Trutnev's proximity to Putin, with Putin. He could buy Trump's villa only if the deal was approved "from above." Without the Kremlin's approval, he could not buy Trump's villa, especially since he was not buying it for himself, or his wife, or his family, but for some other reason. "Rybolovlev always said that he was connected to the KGB, that he had a KGB general who helped him and protected him," a witness recalled. "But if he was connected to the intelligence services, as is suggested, and knowing Rybolovlev, who was quite a clever man—he would never have allowed himself to buy Trump's villa without the authorization of the people at the top."

The KGB general was Ezubchenko, who was Rybolovlev's handler not only in Russia but also abroad. Here is what the Russian Dagestani publication *Chernovik* wrote about Ezubchenko's work in Monaco:

According to unconfirmed official information, General Ezubchenko, both directly and through Dmitry Rybolovlev, negotiated with Prince Albert II of Monaco and representatives of the principality's law enforcement system on the non-extradition and provision of security guarantees to fugitive banker Georgy Bedjamov, former co-owner of

Vneshprombank, which collapsed in 2016, accused of stealing money from the accounts of relatives of Russia's top elite—former head of the presidential administration Sergei Ivanov, Defence Minister Sergei Shoigu, former Deputy Prime Minister Dmitry Kozak and head of state-owned Transneft Nikolai Tokarev. In addition to the families of Ivanov, Kozak, and Shoigu, the country's largest companies, including Rosneft, Rosneftegaz, and Transneft, held accounts at the bankrupt bank. The Russian Olympic Committee and the structures of the Russian Orthodox Church were also affected.

The perpetrators of the embezzlement of billions were quickly identified—the banker's sister Larisa Markus was detained in Moscow, while Georgy Bedjamov managed to flee abroad, but was arrested in Monaco through Interpol. Normally, Monaco is quick and easy to extradite Russian fugitives, but there was a glitch. The court of the Principality first refused to extradite the ex-owner of Vneshprombank, citing health problems, and then released him on bail.

Rumors spread in Monaco and Russia that Russian billionaire Dmitry Rybolovlev was involved in Bedjamov's miraculous release. Well-informed sources confirmed that "Dmitry got seriously involved in this situation", involving all his resources available in the Principality of Monaco and the Kremlin. Allegedly, at the behest of Ezubchenko, an offer was made to Bedjamov through Rybolovlev's corrupt network of law enforcers, which he could not refuse.

In exchange for getting out of prison and ensuring immunity from extradition to Russia, the fugitive undertook to hand over €300 million to Rybolovlev.

The thing is that the deal consisted of two parts. In addition to €300 million, the fugitive banker agreed to hand over to his "salvator" the entire array of confidential data on the use of funds by Vneshprombank's VIP clients. This included all the classified information on transactions to offshore and other accounts of relatives of Kremlin officials. In turn, Rybolovlev passed Bedjamov's dirt to his patrons from the FSB.[21]

The decision on this purchase was made not by Rybolovlev, but by the Russian authorities, namely the Kremlin or the Lubyanka: Rybolovlev received instructions from Moscow to buy Trump's villa saving him from new bankruptcy. When Rybolovlev's wife Elena asked her husband why he had bought the villa, Rybolovlev replied, "I was obliged to do this."

"For tax purposes, the sale price is stated at $95.000.000,"—the bill of sale stated. The total square footage of the structures was 62.000 square feet. The total lot size—6,26 acres. The property was located at 515 North County Road, Palm Beach, Florida[22].

Rybolovlev was not familiar with Trump himself, according to Trump: "'I never met him. He was represented by a broker. I heard a lot of good things about him and his family. He just happened to be from Russia, he's a rich guy from Russia," Trump told Politico in a July 2016 interview.

As part of the conveyance of the Florida property, the parties signed a confidentiality and nondisclosure agreement. The essence of that agreement is not clear and its content is not known. Notably, the information regarding all of the real estate sales in the United States is open to the public under the applicable law. It is possible, of course, to conceal the identity of the purchaser by affecting the purchase through corporate entities and trusts; but it is not possible to hide from the public the fact that the sale itself took place. By the summer of 2008, it became known that Rybolovlev was the purchaser of the Florida property[23], and that fact bothered Rybolovlev a great deal; he blamed "chatty" Trump for disclosing the commercial secret.

Around May-June 2008, Reuters sent an email to Uralkali asking whether Rybolovlev (who was then president of the company's board of directors and its major shareholder) was the buyer of Trump's villa. "I remember that Dmitri considered very carefully the issue with his advisors—did JSC Uralkali have to refuse to comment, or should the company confirm that Dmitri was the purchaser," Elena Rybolovleva told later. "Finally, it was decided that JSC Uralkali's spokesman, Mr. Alan Basiev, would release on behalf of Dmitri a very short statement confirming the purchase, stating that the acquisition was simply an investment in real estate by one of the companies in which Dmitri had an interest, but did not represent a decision of our family to live in the United States."

Rybolovlev stated for Reuters by email through his spokesman the following: "For many years my main business interests have been in the potash industry, but I also have many interests in a range of companies all around the world. These companies operate in different fields of business. In particular, one of them makes investments in real estate. This acquisition is simply an investment in real estate by one of those companies in which I have an interest and does not represent a decision by me to live in the US. Indeed, neither my family nor I have any intention to do so."

However, the purchase of the Palm Beach mansion stood out from Rybolovlev's other property acquisitions. When Rybolovlev bought the property, he always adhered to certain rules: he agreed to the purchase with his wife; he invested in extensive renovation work in each property he bought; he visited the property annually; and he never sold the property at a loss. The case with the Palm Beach mansion was different: his wife strongly disagreed with the idea of buying the house and was not informed about it in advance; Rybolovlev did not invest a cent in the villa after the purchase; he never visited it after the deal was finalized, and sold the property with great difficulty, to unnamed buyers, as land, at a loss to himself. Meanwhile, it was at that time the most expensive property ever bought by Rybolovlev, or perhaps ever sold, in the United States.

It was indeed impossible to resell this villa at a profit and justify the purchase as a property investment. In 2013, Palm Beach County appraised the property and determined its value to be $59,8 million.

In March 2016, Rybolovlev obtained a demolition permit, demolished the villa for an additional $234.000, subdivided the lot into three sub-lots, and listed these for sale the same year at land value.

Each of the three sub-lots listed for sale was a beachfront property. The best one of the three was sold in November 2016 for $34,34 million to a trust managed by a Palm Beach attorney Maura Ziska. The length of the shoreline for that property was 52 meters, while the same length of the shorelines for the other two sub-lots was 46 meters each; that same sub-lot occupied 2,72 acres—i.e., significantly more than a 1/3 of the total acreage of 6,26 acres of the original lot. With that in mind, it seems that the selling price amounted to $12.625 per acre, while the original purchase price of the entire lot at 535 North County Road amounted to $15.175 per acre. Therefore, it looks like Rybolovlev lost money on the sale of the first sub-lot in 2016.

He sold another sub-lot in October 2017 when a Boca Raton attorney Holly G. Gershon, on behalf of 535 North County Road LLC, purchased a 1,97-acre sub-lot for $37 million[24]. On whose behalf attorney Gershon purchased this sub-lot is not entirely clear.

However, by the time Rybolovlev was disposing of the Florida sub-lots, the former owner of the property became the President of the United States, and the overpayment by Rybolovlev of the tens of millions of dollars for that property appeared more and more like a bribe, a credit or an advance.

Now Rybolovlev had to explain to the nosy journalists why he made his purchase, which was no trivial matter. Rybolovlev either did not know it himself since he was acting on the orders from above or he did know but was not at liberty to disclose any details. Therefore, all of his explanations were confusing and unconvincing. He said, for example, that he purchased the villa to ensure that his family had a home in Florida for the years to come; he said also that he made this purchase as an investment and that he was hoping to resell the villa later at a profit; another version voiced by him was that he was planning to demolish the villa from day one and to build a new palace in its stead; finally, he said that he had to demolish the building since it was completely covered in mold.

It is true that if one does not turn on the air conditioning in a vacant building in Florida, mold is inevitable. But this is another fact supporting the suspicion that Rybolovlev must have been completely indifferent to the condition of Trump's villa for which he grossly overpaid. Why would he have thrown away so much money and, according to some sources, made a spectacle of himself in the eyes of those who were even a little bit familiar with the real estate market in the United States? Why was it so important for Rybolovlev to render financial assistance to Trump, thereby rescuing him from bankruptcy?

Rybolovlev completed the acquisition of the Trump's villa on 12 May 2008. It seems that, by that time, the Kremlin had already made a decision to support Trump financially, and Rybolovlev must have been made aware of that fact. Also, in May 2008, Lev Levayev (Leviev), a Russian-born businessman, recruited by the KGB before he emigrated to Israel, came to New York for meetings with Trump. The subject matter of the discussions was never made public. It was stated that no agreements were reached between the parties concerning any joint projects in Russia.

However, members of the Trump family started visiting Moscow so frequently during 2007-2008 that tracking their comings and goings had become challenging. In 2008, Donald Trump Jr. stated that he visited Russia six times over the previous eighteen months, which meant he had flown there once every three months.

While before his first trip of 2007-2008, Donald Trump, according to his tweet in July 2007, had "zero investments in Russia," the situation had changed significantly by the last trip of that period, when on 4 June 2008, in the middle of a financial crisis in the US, Donald Trump Jr. participated in the "Real Estate in Russia" conference organized in Moscow by the Adam Smith Institute. As part of his keynote speech, he described the plans for elite residential real estate and hotel construction in Moscow, St. Petersburg, and Sochi. He added that the Trump Organization was not considering any real estate development projects in the US at the moment, but instead, it was focusing on strengthening its brand in the "global market," which included real estate development projects in Panama, Seoul, Honolulu, Istanbul, Dominical Republic, Dubai, and Russia. "Compared to a stagnation in the US real estate market, a recent 50% increase in Russia of a price per square meter was a revelation for me," concluded Donald Trump-Jr. hoping for a miracle.

The miracle happened, and Rybolovlev was not the only one. Donald Trump collected a lot of Russian money. In September 2008 Donald Trump-Jr. pointed out at the Manhattan Real Estate Conference that now "Russians make up a pretty disproportionate cross-section of a lot of our assets... We see a lot of money pouring in from Russia". He added that he preferred Moscow "over all cities in the world".[25]

For the sake of completeness, this quote should be supplemented by a few more quotes (even though these came a few years later). The first one was Michael Cohen's story to Rachel Maddow on 24 December 2020 in a lengthy interview with the American TV channel MSNBC, where Cohen explained lucidly that the $50 million overpaid by Rybolovlev for a mansion in Florida, according to Trump, was Putin's money, and that the instruction to Rybolovlev to buy the mansion from Trump was given by Putin himself, as well as instructions to all other oligarchs to invest in Trump[26].

The second is Bouvier's opinion that Rybolovlev received the authorization to invest in Trump "from the very top", and without it, Rybolovlev wouldn't have risked doing business with Trump.

Then, there are words by the head of the Department of Urban

Development for the City of Moscow in March-April 2016: "We invested so much in Trump that he has no chance of losing".[27]

Finally, an email written by Felix Sater, "Our boy can become president of the USA and we can engineer it. I will get all of Putin's team to buy in on this, I will manage this process.[28]"

Since 2008, the process started moving. In 2009, Trump changed his voter registration from Democrat to Republican. He seriously considered running for President as a Republican in 2012. In May 2011, he decided not to run but proclaimed: "I maintain a strong conviction that if I were to run, I would be able to win the primary and, ultimately, the general election."[29]

In 2012, Trump again registered as a Republican and publicly endorsed Republican Presidential nominee Mitt Romney for president. Romney lost to the Democrat Barack Obama.

If not 2012, then 2016. Trump's Presidency in the Kremlin's eyes was just a question of time, during which he should be encouraged to develop a closer relationship with the Kremlin—especially since he was not against it. In January 2013, rumors started that Trump was looking into potentially buying *The New York Times*[30].

In the United States, everyone thought of this rumor as a tasteless joke since a businessman on the brink of bankruptcy would not seem to be able to afford such an expensive purchase. Indeed, Trump seems to have been considering the purchase of one of the premier US newspapers, which could become the main informational tool in his Presidential Campaign of 2016. But this project was not realized back in 2013. It was revisited in Moscow after Trump won the Presidency, when the mainstream press in the US started criticizing Trump because of the suspected Russian interference in the 2016 US Presidential election and because Trump refused to acknowledge the interference. In January 2017, the Kremlin suggested that the Russian oligarchs execute the acquisition of *The New York Times*, probably considering it the most straightforward, efficient, and inexpensive way to suppress Trump's critics.

But let us return to 2013. Trump decided to hold in Russia the Miss Universe Pageant. For the future candidate for the US Presidency, it was a calculated political and financial move, which was by no means random or reckless. Trump was trying to build bridges with his new and important strategic ally—Putin. The Miss Universe Pageant was one of such bridges.

A final decision regarding this matter was made in mid-June 2013 in Las Vegas during Trump's meeting with Aras Agalarov (and his family, including his son, Emin, the future moderator of the Pageant). Aras Agalarov, a Russian billionaire, happened to be the main Russian sponsor of the Pageant[31]. From the US side, the meeting was attended also by Rob Goldston, a musical producer responsible for organizing the Pageant in Moscow.

On the next day, Trump started trying to set up his first meeting with Putin. On 18 June 2013, a soon-to-be Republican Party Presidential Candidate wrote on Twitter: "Do you think Putin will be going to the Miss Universe Pageant in November in Moscow—and if so, will he become my best friend?"[32]

Intended for Putin's eyes and ears, it was an invitation to meet with Trump.

Aras Agalarov recalled that Trump was completely fixated on the idea of meeting with Putin in November, and Agalarov, of course, promised to facilitate the meeting. In October, Trump asked Agalarov to look into this once more, Agalarov called someone—supposedly Putin's press secretary, Dmitri Peskov, and again attempted to set up the November Trump-Putin meeting[33].

Putin seems to have "heard" Trump and on 29 October 2013, i.e. just a couple of weeks after Agalarov's fussy phone calls, Putin personally presented the Order of Honor to Aras Agalarov. At that time, Agalarov had no services to the Russian state other than meeting Trump and funding the Miss Universe pageant, part of the budget that went into Trump's pocket. But by that time Trump had managed to "gaffe" in one of his TV interviews—on late-night David Letterman's 17 October 2013 show—that Putin was a "tough guy" and that he had "met him once."[34]

If this is true, the meeting was completely secret and was not reported to anyone, nor was the content of their conversation or the agreements known. On the contrary, it was publicly reported that Trump wrote a letter to Putin inviting him to attend the pageant, hinting that it would be an opportunity to see hordes of beautiful girls. But Putin, they say, did not come to the contest and did not meet with Trump then, but sent him a gift and a letter. Did Putin meet with Trump then or not?

On 9-10 November, Agalarov and Trump held the Miss Universe

Pageant at the Crocus City Hall just outside of Moscow, which was owned by Agalarov. Trump was paid a $12,2 million fee for participating in the Pageant and was pleased with the hospitality he received in Moscow: "When I went to Russia with the Miss Universe pageant, [Putin] contacted me and was so nice. I mean, the Russian people were so fantastic to us."[35]

Herman Gref who had served in various key roles in the Russian Government, including that of a Chairman of Sberbank of Russia organized a get-together with a dozen of powerful Russian businessmen. "I called it my weekend in Moscow," Trump reminisced in September 2015. "I spent some time with the top-level people—oligarchs, military personnel, top government officials. I cannot go into too much detail but I will tell you that I met with some very important people and was treated extraordinarily."

"I do have a relationship [with Putin],"—Trump said,—"and I can tell you that he's very interested in what we're doing here today. He's probably very interested in what you and I are saying today and I'm sure he's going to be seeing it in some form. But I do have a relationship with him and I think it's very interesting to see what's happened. I mean, look, he's done a very brilliant job in terms of what he represents and who he's representing. If you look at what he's done with Syria, if you look at so many of the different things, he has eaten our president's lunch, let's not kid ourselves."[36]

The feeling was mutual. However, we are aware of that fact solely based on Trump's own words, who said during his Presidential Campaign in June 2016 that Putin "said one nice thing about me. He said I'm a genius."[37] Brief and modest.

"I do have plans to establish business in Russia. I am currently in negotiations with several Russian companies regarding skyscraper construction," Trump stated in an interview on 9 November 2013, while refusing to divulge any specifics.

On 11 November 2013, Trump and his business partners from the Trump SoHo Development, Alex Sapir and Rotem Rosen, met with Aras Agalarov to discuss potential real estate development projects. Among the discussion topics were plans to build a 58-floor hotel in Moscow. "The Russian market is attracted to me. I have a great relationship with many Russians, and almost all of the oligarchs were in the room,"—stated Trump in an interview to *Real Estate Weekly* on 12 November 2013, upon returning from Russia[38].

This was Trump's third attempt to enter the Russian real estate market after the attempts of 2004 and 2007-2008. As we know, none of these projects were realized. Nevertheless, Trump was very pleased with his trip to Russia and on 12 November personally thanked the Agalarov family via Twitter: "I had a great weekend with you and your family. You have done a fantastic job. Trump-tower-Moscow is next. Emin was wow!" "We had an awesome time Trump-tower-Moscow—let's make it happen!" Emin responded[39].

"It" did not happen. What happened was completely different: in June 2015, Trump officially declared that he was running for a President from the Republican Party. At that moment, Rybolovlev realized that this was his big break and that he would be able to receive a return, with interest, on his $95 million investment from 2008.

4

Yves Bouvier and the World's Freeports

By this time, Rybolovlev's position in Russia and abroad had strengthened considerably. In June 2010, Rybolovlev sold his stake in Uralkali to oligarch Suleiman Kerimov for billions of dollars. On 22 May 2012, Rybolovlev's partner Trutnev was appointed as an aide to President Putin and, in this connection, handed over the mandate of Member of the State Duma to his fellow countryman A. G. Lomakin, a billionaire who got rich from the sale of Uralkali, Silvinist, and Belaruskali potash fertilizers.

On 31 August 2013, Trutnev also became Deputy Prime Minister of Russia and Plenipotentiary Representative of the President of Russia in the Far Eastern Federal District.

Ezubchenko served as deputy head of the Presidential Administration (PA) of the Russian Federation from 2005-2011, became deputy director of the Federal Security Service (FSB) from 2018-2020, acting head of the FSB Economic Security Service from 2020-2021, and in 2021—first deputy head of the FSB's Internal Security Department and, in addition, deputy chief of staff of the Security Council of the Russian Federation. He has been deputy to all of Russia's top government officials.

In the early 2000s, Rybolovlev, Trutnev, and Ezubchenko were consumed by one super-idea: the creation of their own Freeport—a tax-free harbor for trading diamonds and "everything" in general—gold, weapons, anything—through Freeports, bypassing the SWIFT banking system.

On their first visit to Monaco, Trutnev and Rybolovlev thought about the idea of opening a Freeport there. It seemed easy to establish a Freeport in Monaco, where Rybolovlev had settled and acquired high-ranking connections. But he had to talk to "number one", not "number five"; he had to get close to the top leadership of the country: to the president in Russia; to the Prime Minister of England, Tony Blair (during the auction where Tony Blair was, he bought a lot to draw attention to himself, and then hired Tony Blair's brother as his lawyer); in America, he bought Trump's villa...

To get closer to Prince Albert II of Monaco, who became head of state in April 2005, and at the same time to get in an accelerated order of Monegasque citizenship, Rybolovlev bought in December 2011, 66,7% of the football club AS Monaco, owned by the ruling family Grimaldi in the Principality. The club was bought through the Zeus Trust, which was managed by Andreas Neocleous, of the law firm Andreas Neocleous & Co LLC[40]. This firm specializes in international trusts. Rybolovlev became the firm's most high-profile client.

A third of the club remained in the ownership of the Prince of Monaco. The amount of the deal was not disclosed. However, there was nothing to disclose. Rybolovlev purchased the club for €1 but pledged to invest at least €100 million. Indeed, over the years, he invested more than that—i.e., approximately €300 million, buying several players and thereby making a weak team successful.

Football was the Prince of Monaco's favorite game, and Albert II, along with Rybolovlev and his daughter Catherine, became regular attendees at the football club's games, meeting in the stadium box several times a year. This investment became a springboard for Rybolovlev to connect with the royal family and close contacts with ministers, MPs, and police officials who provided him with insider information and even drafted legislation that favored his interests.

Meetings with Prince Albert also took place outside the stadium. In June 2014, Albert II traveled to Rybolovlev's house to celebrate the birthday of Rybolovlev's daughter Ekaterina. The birthday was celebrated on the Greek island of Skorpios, owned by Rybolovlev[41].

In July 2014, Albert II visited a villa in Rio de Janeiro rented by Rybolovlev for the 2014 FIFA World Cup in Brazil. In August 2016, Albert II spent a day aboard Rybolovlev's yacht anchored in the Mediterranean Sea off the French island of Corsica. In 2017, Albert II holidayed at Rybolovlev's estate in Mallorca. In August 2021, Rybolovlev's yacht won the Rolex Fastnet Race and he presented the trophy to Prince Albert II in

September 2021. Albert was invited to Rybolovlev's birthday celebration in Namibia in November 2021 but was unable to attend for personal reasons. In September 2022, Prince Albert II opened the new sports complex together with Rybolovlev's daughter Ekaterina and her husband Juan Sartori[42].

Over time, the heads of the security services became Rybolovlev's "favorites" in Monaco: Principality Police Chief Régis Asso, Justice Minister Philippe Narmino and Interior Minister Paul Masseron (who in February 2011 received bottles of alcohol worth several thousand euros from Rybolovlev as a gift, which went beyond the "year-end" gifts allowed by law). Rybolovlev was granted a residence permit in Monaco shortly thereafter. And on 4 April 2015, Masseron stepped down and joined AS Monaco as an "advisor" to Rybolovlev[43].

With such connections, the Monaco Freeport seemed almost in his pocket. But when the project was presented to the Monaco authorities, they scrutinized it and did everything themselves, without Rybolovlev. So, the Freeport in Monaco was, indeed, opened with money from the Monaco state, but Rybolovlev and Trutnev had nothing to do with it. Another initiator of the project, businessman Yves Bouvier, was also ousted from the project.

Yet, the idea of creating Freeports belonged not to Rybolovlev or Trutnev or even to Putin, but to a Swiss businessman Yves Bouvier, who already created such Freeports in Geneva, Luxembourg and Singapore. Actually, the first Freeport was created in Geneva in 1888 and became legendary. But Bouvier, having inherited from his father Natural Le Coultre, a transportation company, back in 1997, which was purchased by his father in 1982, became the first one who apply the concept of Freeport to the transportation and storage of art objects and other valuables. Over time, Bouvier took upon himself the entire scope of operations concerning the acquisition and disposition of art objects by individuals and companies, including handling the underlying financial transactions. "I saw how the dealers worked," Bouvier recalled. "With a good network and know-how, they could make a fortune on a single sale. I was no dumber than anyone else, and I had everyone's trust. And I told myself that this business was much more profitable than transport."

The Geneva Freeport, which was holding an estimated $100 billion works of art, was not the property of Bouvier. Bouvier's company Natural

Le Coultre simply leased 20.000 square meters of space in the port (out of 130.000 square meters of total floor space) and was considered to own 5% of the "port." 85% was owned by the Canton of Geneva, where the "port" was located. 10% were owned by others. It was subject to Swiss laws, which became less and less favorable to tax-avoiding customers. Finally, it was too expensive. It costs the client $1000 a month to store one medium-sized painting. Monthly rent for a small room costs $5.000 to $12.000.

By the time Rybolovlev was introduced to Bouvier in August 2002, while he was picking up at the Freeport in Geneva his first painting ("Circus" by Marc Chagall) that he purchased for €6 million, Bouvier was well-known in an inner circle of those trading in art masterpieces. "Rybolovlev was tense," Bouvier later recalled. "He was not given a certificate of authenticity for the painting. He was afraid of being cheated. I did for him what was necessary."

However, Bouvier attracted Rybolovlev not as an art dealer, which Bouvier wasn't. He attracted Rybolovlev as a partner, through whom he could broaden the network of Freeports to include Vladivostok, which was monitored by Trutnev. With that in mind, Rybolovlev set out to befriend Bouvier. From Rybolovlev's viewpoint, this was solely a business undertaking, which could be implemented by the infusion of significant capital. For Bouvier, Rybolovlev was just a client—a very rich client, a lottery ticket worth hundreds of millions of dollars.

As relevant to this book, Bouvier is interesting for two reasons. One side of his life is well-known: he became Rybolovlev's art dealer, after the two have met in Geneva in August 2002. Notably, this aspect was kept secret for a long time by both Bouvier and Rybolovlev. The former was not keen on disclosing the fact that he had a rich—a very rich—a fantastically rich—client. The latter was not keen on making public his numerous purchases of the art objects since, as was the case with the purchase of the Trump villa, he was purchasing these for private reasons which seemed to have nothing to do with displaying art and admiring its beauty.

But neither was Bouvier an ordinary seller nor was Rybolovlev a typical buyer. A true collector of paintings never relies on one dealer or broker but he also hires an expert with whom he consults and whom he trusts, he also spends time attending numerous auctions, in person or virtually. He typically takes an active part in selecting the paintings for purchase. In contrast, Rybolovlev handled everything through Bouvier, and, according to Bouvier,

Rybolovlev took a couple of minutes in deciding whether to purchase any given painting. And this approach should really make us think whether Rybolovlev was interested in art or had other objectives which had nothing to do with art.

"In my life I will invest in three areas: the stock exchange, property and art objects, because this is where the price always increases over time. With paintings, I also have the advantage that if I have a problem, I can take them on a plane and leave with them," Rybolovlev said. Sometimes Rybolovlev bought a painting from a photograph. Sometimes, as it seemed at least to Bouvier, he would show him three photographs of three different master-pieces, and Rybolovlev would immediately choose the best quality photo-graph where the painting could be seen better. Sometimes the photographs of the selected works were printed life-size to try them on the walls (on which, let us emphasize again, these paintings never appeared).

Bouvier said he knew of no client who had not looked at the original painting before buying it, or sent a curator from a museum and based his decision on a photograph.

Usually, a collector, when hundreds of millions of dollars are involved, doesn't make quick decisions. It was different with Rybolovlev. Bouvier would bring Rybolovlev to a masterpiece, and he would ask, "How much?" Bouvier would name a price. "All right," Rybolovlev replied.—Everything else—discuss it with Sazonov." The deal was finalized in five minutes, and as a rule, the matter was never revisited.

Rybolovlev never signed any documents himself. Everything was handled through Sazonov who assumed all of the financial and tax risks of any given transaction. Sazonov had once been an employee of the Russian Federal Tax Service and then joined Rybolovlev's Uralkali. Rybolovlev believed that Sazonov was assigned to him by Ezubchenko through the FSB. Bouvier believed the same. Since the Russian tax service was under the juris-diction of the KGB/FSB, Sazonov's cooperation with state security was a natural thing.

Sazonov held various positions at Uralkali. He was CEO of Uralkali Trading Gibraltar (2007) and director of Uralkali Trading SA (July 2005—September 2010). But, in addition, he assumed all risks for possible financial or tax irregularities. He was a director of numerous trusts and companies owned by Rybolovlev: Philodice Holding Limited (Cyprus), Xitrans Finance

LTD (British Virgin Islands), Bovingdon Holding Limited (Cyprus), Ribovax Biotechnologies SA (Switzerland), White Garden SA (Switzerland), Destrieto Investment SA (Panama). He was also president of Rybolovlev's company Aquagem Investment SA (Panama) and CEO of Xigen SA (Switzerland).

Sazonov was the only one who could independently sign bank accounts and control all financial flows. All communication between Sazonov and Rybolovlev was verbal (Rybolovlev did not even have a personal e-mail account, and he very rarely used anything related to electronic communication). Sazonov's email address was used for correspondence. Contracts for paintings bought from Bouvier listed Sazonov as the final buyer.

According to Bouvier, Sazanov never asked for a cut or a bribe—Bouvier thinks that he was too afraid for his life to do that.

Sazonov was deathly afraid of Rybolovlev, because he knew exactly what Rybolovlev did and was doing, and he realized that Rybolovlev was dangerous. But Rybolovlev was also wary of Sazonov, a man who never looked his interlocutor in the eyes, because the latter had stayed with Rybolovlev for too long and was aware of all his financial transactions.

"Sazonov was a very erudite man," Bouvier recalls of him. "He had a huge library of books, and he read them from morning to night. One day I asked him to recommend me some serious books on China. The next day, Sazonov sent me a list of 30 books."

My attempts to meet with Mikhail Sazonov, who lives in France, not far from Geneva, were not successful, and it makes sense: Sazonov must be the weakest link in the financial side of Rybolovlev's business since all of the financial documentation was completed and signed by Sazonov. While not necessarily a privy to Rybolovlev's and Trutnev's strategic planning, Sazonov was well-informed about the Rybolovlev's cash flows.

I managed to speak with Sazonov by phone from Geneva on 2 June 2018, and we spoke for 22 minutes. Sazonov said that he has not worked with Rybolovlev for two years, that he has not given any interviews in the past and that he does not want to start doing that in the future. I tried to convince Sazonov to meet with me in person; I told him openly and in detail what specifically interested me in connection with Rybolovlev; I relayed to him the main thesis of the publication that was planned; and at his request, I sent him the list of questions I wanted to ask, in response to which I received a reply: "I have no knowledge regarding the majority of the topics you raised. Therefore, I have nothing to tell you and see no point in us meeting." That was the end of my attempts to communicate further with Sazonov.

My modest attempt to meet with Rybolovlev himself that I tried to arrange through his press-secretary, Sergei Chernitsyn, has likewise failed, as did an attempt to reach his now-ex-wife Elena, who is precluded from providing any information or giving interviews in accordance with the terms of her divorce settlement. Thus, it looks that Rybolovlev succeeded in erecting around himself a serious information wall.

Rybolovlev always was very careful. The purchases were made with serious precautions. Payments were made into the account of MEI Invest Limited, a Hong Kong company owned by Bouvier. The original owner of the works was never specified (one of the main rules of any art dealer was not to name the source of receipt of goods). After the purchase, ownership rights were registered in the name of Virgin Islands-based entities (Xitrans Finance, then Accent Delight). No contracts were usually signed. In addition to the sums paid for the paintings, the seller (Bouvier) sent the buyer (Rybolovlev) invoices for "various services and due diligence in connection with the acquisition": transport, insurance, expertise, delivery of the title deed, etc. The amount of these expenses was 2% of the value of the masterpieces.

It is known that none of the paintings he bought Rybolovlev did not hang on the walls of any of his houses. And these houses were many: in Monaco La Villa Hermosa at 9 Boulevard de Suisse, (sold in 2010) and villa La Belle Epoque at 15-17 Avenue d'Ostende, bought in 2010 for $308 million; in Geneva villa Chemin des Princes 24 at Cologne, bought in 2002 and sold in 2015 due to the Bouvier scandal; two chalets in the high Swiss resort town of Gstaad at Alpinastrasse 23, bought in 2013 for $260 million; a penthouse in New York City at 15 Central Park West, bought in 2012 for $88 million for daughter Catherine (the 10-room flat had 6700 sq. ft. of living space and 2000 sq. ft. of terrace); a beach property in Hawaii, purchased in December 2011 for $20 million; a penthouse at 20 Grosvenor Square in London, purchased in 2022 for £50,5 million; a villa in Valpheres, St Tropez, France, purchased for €60 million; a mansion bordering the Elysee Palace, the residence of the president, and once owned by the last

French empress Eugenie, wife of Napoleon III, in the 8th arrondissement of Paris, bought in 2008 for €21,5 million, sold in November 2020; a property on the Palm Jumeirah, an artificial archipelago in Dubai, bought for $29,5 million.

And finally, the 74-acre Skorpios Island was purchased in April 2013 from Athina Onassis, granddaughter of Greek tycoon Aristotle Onassis. The island itself cost Rybolovlev $154 million, with additional investments totaling €184 million. The island became a luxurious private resort and was even adapted for discreet mooring of submarines, which was used, according to the security guards, to organize secret high-level visits that should not be known to outsiders.

Nowhere on the walls of Rybolovlev's properties hung the works of art he purchased, including Da Vinci's *Salvator Mundi*. None of the visitors to Rybolovlev's numerous estates have ever seen a single painting in his house. Could it be that these paintings never belonged to Rybolovlev and this was the reason why he had no right and desire to hang them?

Once he saw in the house of an American businessman in New York, also related to the potash business, a painting by Claude Monet's *Nymphaea (Lilies)* and asked Bouvier to buy for him two such paintings of the same size (Monet painted many *Lilies*), to raise in the eyes of the American partner of his status. But even these paintings he did not hang on the walls.

However, when discussing the construction of a new house, which was never built, Rybolovlev asked the architect to design it taking into account the paintings that he planned to hang. Bouvier, who took part in this discussion, allowed himself to joke: "Please, make a lot of empty walls, so that one could hang many paintings."

In August 2003, a year after having met Rybolovlev, Bouvier sold to him the first painting—Vincent van Gogh's *Paysage Avec un Olivier*, from the collection of Pierre Bergé and Yves Saint Laurent, for $17 million.

However, the "first pancake" on the sale of Van Gogh to Rybolovlev turned out to be a "failure".

Bouvier had other clients, including people from Russia, bringing Bouvier a good profit. In the art world, agreements were usually made verbally. When negotiating the price, and the parties came to an agreement, it meant that even without a signed paper, the seller was obliged to sell the painting for the agreed price, and the buyer—to buy. This is how they behaved, including rich Russian clients who bought paintings from Bouvier. Once the price was agreed, it did not change, and any written agreements were then formalized based on this verbal agreement.

Bouvier offered Rybolovlev Van Gogh for $20 million. Rybolovlev agreed (as reflected in their correspondence). But Rybolovlev asked for a delay in payment: he had no money to spare at the time. Van Gogh on the road is not lying, and while Bouvier waited for payment, another of his clients offered to buy the painting for the same $20 million immediately. At the same time, Sotheby's Auctioneers offered to buy the painting for a guaranteed $17 million, plus a premium for a future sale at auction, which could mean a profit of much more than $20 million, depending on the outcome of the auction. Rybolovlev reiterated the $20 million price for now but again asked for a delay.

Bouvier took a risk. He turned down Sotheby's and a second client offering $20 million and waited patiently for Rybolovlev's decision. Unexpectedly, Rybolovlev offered as his final terms $17 million and three months' grace period. Since Bouvier had already turned down all other potential buyers, he was forced to accept Rybolovlev's offer.

This was a good lesson, and Bouvier negotiated all subsequent deals differently. He named a price and never lowered it again. In four cases, after Rybolovlev refused to agree to the price, Bouvier sold the paintings to other buyers, and more expensive than the price Rybolovlev named. Whether it was a coincidence that Rybolovlev reduced the price from $20 million to $17 million, i.e. to the price offered by Sotheby's, or whether someone informed Rybolovlev of this price and that Bouvier had already refused all other potential buyers, we can only guess. Bouvier had no free money at the time. To keep painting for which he already paid Bouvier could not afford. Giving away painting for $17 million Bouvier would still have a profit. So, in the end, Rybolovlev got Van Gogh for $17 million.

There was another consideration. A subtle psychologist Bouvier realized that he was dealing with a new very rich buyer who wanted to build his collection and decorate the walls of his expensive house with expensive masterpieces. With this first sale, he was ready to "lose" $3 million because the work with this new client could continue and bring new sales. As for the future, now Bouvier never agreed to reduce the price. He would bargain with Rybolovlev concerning installments on payments for the purchased paintings but not about the price of the masterpieces.

Thereafter, Bouvier put in place a cunning strategy to ensure that Rybolovlev would not renegotiate the agreed price of paintings and sculptures. Like real estate dealers do, he pretended to Sazanov that he was negotiating with the seller to get the best price. Therefore, there was no more space for Sazanov to ask an additional discount to Bouvier. As a result, Bouvier was able to sell all the pieces of art at the price he agreed each time with Rybolovlev and not re-negotiations took place, as the exception of the very last painting by Rothko.

However, these fake negotiations would later on haunt Bouvier as Rybolovlev's lawyers used these exchanges of emails to try to demonstrate to prosecutors and courts all around the world—without success—that Bouvier was not an art dealer but just an agent.

It is hardly a coincidence that in 2004, shortly after Bouvier sold his first painting to Rybolovlev, Bouvier launched an art fair in Moscow with Elena Rybolovlev acting as the co-founder of the event. In 2005, the fair was attended by 50.000 people and was consecrated by the patriarch. A gala was held in the Kremlin. All of this was organized by Rybolovlev. These projects had nothing to do with any art brokerage services or with the logistics of transportation and storage of art pieces. It was an entirely new page in Bouvier's professional activity—the big business and big politics, into which he was being dragged by Rybolovlev who was strategically "befriending" Bouvier.

Over time Bouvier got to know all the ministers of the Russian government and heads of political parties, oligarchs, and people from Alfa-Bank. The events were widely covered by the press and television. One day Bouvier "privatized the Kremlin" to gather thirty oligarchs for a party for which the Moscow government blocked the road to Manezhnaya Square and Tverskaya Street which led to Kremlin.

For his contribution to Russian culture, he was awarded the Pushkin Medal by President Dmitry Medvedev, then also the Fine Arts Medal. In Paris, he met with the Russian ambassador. Since all prominent foreigners were prosecuted in Russia, he knew that he had been scrutinized from head to toe by the Russian authorities and was recognized as a friend of Russia, contributing to the improvement of the investment climate. In 2006, with a local partner, Bouvier set up a transport company in Russia. He rented his depots for storage under the Cathedral of Christ the Salvator, rightly considering it the safest place in Moscow and Russia. "There was no safer place," Bouvier laughed. His bureau and offices were on Manezhnaya Square. On his business card it was written: "Manezhnaya Square, No. 1." He brought $2 billion worth of artwork into Russia for sale. And all this without knowing Russian, with no Russian partners (except for a partner in a transport company), and without paying a single bribe in all those years.

"It was a special time," Bouvier recounted. "In 2004-2008, for foreigners, Russia was the place where you had to come, where you had to be because that's where the biggest parties were held. Everything was happening there. But from an administrative point of view, it became more and more difficult every year. In 2004, you needed one stamp. In 2008, four seals were needed. I thought that this part of Russia would open up—bigger, faster, and become part of big Europe, up to the Urals. But I began to notice that little by little it was closing down. And then it became a headache. And then—it's just a big headache and there's nothing left but a headache. When you have all these exhibitions, when you organize events, you have a certain responsibility and pressure. You're not allowed to make a mistake. And you get a lot of grey hairs. And in 2008 I stopped doing all that."

By this time, the nature of Rybolovlev and Bouvier's relationship had changed. Until 2007, Bouvier was a service provider, a man who sold him paintings. In 2007 Rybolovlev began to have serious problems with his wife Elena, which ended in divorce. On 22 December 2008 in Geneva Elena filed for divorce which was called by the international press the most expensive and scandalous divorce in history. In the process of this divorce which became very ugly, Elena was prepared to share half of the money she would have received from Rybolovlev with her husband's enemy Igor Sechin if Sechin would agree to help her sign an agreement satisfactory to Elena, which Rybolovlev refused to sign.

It is not known whether Sechin and Elena met, but it is known that she did everything to make sure that the meeting took place. Anyway, Sechin did not risk getting involved, and Rybolovlev said that he would never forgive his wife for such a betrayal. And he did not.

Without going into details about the reasons for this divorce, we note that the French proverb "look for a woman" most likely explains what happened. Rybolovlev was interested in girls, and this was known. Putin even once advised Rybolovlev to invest money in the restoration of a monastery and open a women monastery there, to which Rybolovlev joked that he would like to be buried in a women monastery cemetery so that he could be closer to girls in the next world. Rybolovlev did not believe in either God or the devil and was a convinced atheist, but he was superstitious, so he gave money to the church, consecrated his houses and yacht, and used the services of shamans...

In Monaco Rybolovlev opened a ballet school for girls, including those coming from Russia. The ballet school was supervised by Rybolovlev's lawyer Tetiana Bersheda, a Ukrainian-Swiss lawyer living in Monaco. She was born on 24 April 1984 and was the daughter of Ukrainian politician, public figure, and diplomat Eugene Bersheda. His highest position was as Ukraine's ambassador to Switzerland. He resigned in May 2010, possibly due to suspicions that he was recruited by Russian military intelligence (GRU).

Bersheda studied at the University of Fribourg (Switzerland) and the University of Cambridge (England). She is a member of the Geneva Bar and heads her boutique law firm, Bersheda Law, which has branches in Lausanne (1 rue du Grand-Chêne), Geneva (Rue Rodolphe-Toepffer 8) and London (1 Knightsbridge Green). She started working for Rybolovlev as his lawyer in 2009 and became Rybolovlev's close advisor, translator, and confidante, joining the board of directors of AS Monaco Football Club and Monaco Sports Invest (MSI), the company through which Rybolovlev managed the football club. She also handled legal matters for Rybolovlev's family office in Monaco (Rigmora Holdings Ltd.), which had about 20 employees.

On the Russian side, Trutnev, whose personal life raised some questions because Trutnev's third wife, Natalia Sergeevna Petrova, whom he married in 2006, was exceptionally young, was involved in this effort to set up a ballet school in Monaco: Rybolovlev said that when she met Trutnev (who was 50 in 2006) the girl was about 14-15 years old. She was a ballerina. For a while Trutnev led a double life: his second wife Marina Lvovna Trutnev with their two children (Alexander and Dmitry) stayed to live in Perm, where she had a clothing shop. Trutnev and his future (third) wife lived in Moscow. When she became pregnant, Trutnev brought her to Geneva to live with Rybolovlev, and she gave birth to her children in Geneva. A little later, Trutnev formalized his marriage with Natalia. With his second wife and children, he remained on good terms.

Parties with young girls, including underage girls (according to some witness reports), were organized quite often on Rybolovlev's yacht. Some girls lived on the yacht and those were asked to undergo medical check-ups to make sure they were not infected.

Rybolovlev later claimed that his wife knew about it and turned a blind eye for years. Elena later stated in court that the basis for the divorce, was her husband's infidelity, in particular, the fact that her husband was taking girls on an "industrial scale" on the "family yacht". One night, by chance, Elena saw on her husband's unplugged computer information with passport details of the girls invited, including the girl who was Rybolovlev's mistress at the time. A few weeks after this discovery, Elena filed divorce papers, because, on that fateful night, Elena learned that her husband had sex with underage girls[44].

The plot with the "Rybolovlev girls" living on the yacht has its backstory.

In 1999, a man with an interesting biography—Vadim Vasiliev—became the Director of Expertise at Uralkali. He was born on 23 September 1965 into a family of Russian diplomats. In 1987, he graduated from the elite MGIMO Institute, which traditionally trains Russian diplomats and intelligence officers, with a degree in economics. From 1987 to 1990, Vasiliev worked for the USSR Ministry of Foreign Affairs (MFA).

In 1987, shortly after graduating from the institute, he was sent to work at the Soviet embassy in Iceland. In 1990 he returned to Moscow and worked for a year in the central office of the Foreign Ministry, and was connected with the Russian intelligence services, but it is not known whether he was a Soviet intelligence officer.

In 1991-1992, when the USSR collapsed, Vasiliev left the civil service to work for the state foreign trade association Kaliy VAO Agrokhimexport, whose director was A. G. Lomakin.

From 1993 to 1997 Vasiliev was vice-president of Transammonia AG and director of its Moscow representative office, and then export director at Uralkali.

In 2002, he left this position to head Point Model Management, a modeling agency registered on 24 September 2001 in Moscow and located at 60 Bolshaya Gruzinskaya Street, flat 1. The company existed at least until the end of 2014.

Modeling agencies in Russia were a specific business supplying girls to modeling companies, but not only there, offering elite prostitution services to influential politicians and businessmen, Russian and foreign. They were the most important tool in creating, obtaining, and using the kompromat necessary for the subsequent blackmail. For these reasons in Russia, all model agencies were always under the close attention and control of the Russian special services.

Vasiliev was the general director of the modeling agency from 2002 to 2005. The founders of the company were Alexander Shashkov and Maxim Zadubrovsky[45].

In 2005, the ownership structure of the modeling agency was as follows: Centre of Innovations and Technologies had 70% of shares and Zadubrovsky CJSC had 30%. As of 16 March 2015, the structure of the company changed to Centre of Innovations and Technologies (99%) and Tatyana Grigorieva (1%). But the sole owner of the Centre for Innovations and Technologies, located at 60 Bolshaya Gruzinskaya Street, Moscow, flat 1 (i.e. the same address where the modeling agency was registered), was Yuri Babich, who was also the head of Uralkali's Moscow office.

Zadubrovsky began his career as a male model with Vyacheslav Zaitsev, a well-known fashion designer at the time. Zadubrovsky was also the director of Zaitsev's modeling agency, which was established in 1993 and was part of another modeling agency, Red Stars.

Red Stars was founded by Vitaly Leiba, the leader of an "Abkhazian" organized crime group, and Arigon, a British company owned by Semyon Mogilevich, a Russian intelligence agent and criminal mastermind operating mainly out of Austria. Mogilevich was one of the main links between Russian intelligence and the criminal underworld in Russia and abroad. In the early 1990s, when Leyba and Mogilevich were living in Hungary, the Red Stars were run by former Soviet model Tatyana Koltsova. She was directly involved in Mogilevich's operations, including scams involving large sums of money from the Central Bank of Russia, laundering criminal proceeds, and organizing elite prostitution in Western Europe, mainly in Germany and France.

Zadubrovsky was a liaison between Leyba and Zaitsev's modeling agency. However, in 1999, due to the deteriorating reputation of Red Stars, Leiba founded another modeling agency—President Model Management—

where Zadubrovsky became the president.

In 2001 Rybolovlev decided to create his modeling agency Modus Vivendis and hired managers, including Zadubrovsky, from President Model Management to run it.

Rybolovlev was reverent and even morbid about this part of his business. For example, on 13 July 2015, Bersheda signed a contract with Peter Garske, director of the private London detective agency Arcanum, for $1 million a month to spy on Rybolovlev's girlfriend elite model Daria Strokous[46]. So, the girls on the yacht that angered Elena Rybolovleva was not a random event.

Because of the two investigations—the Sechin and divorce investigations—Rybolovlev was rightly afraid that the Swiss government would cooperate with the Russian prosecutor's office, and Elena would have his property seized, as she could presumably claim half of the jointly acquired property. There was a lot of property, including paintings.

In October 2004, Bouvier acquired *Les Noces de Pierrette* by Picasso from the Manhattan art dealer William Acquavella and re-sold it to Rybolovlev for $43,8 million. The volume of sales started growing over time. Between 2003 and 2007, Bouvier sold 6 art masterpieces to Rybolovlev, whereas between 2008 and 2013, he sold 28. In June 2008, he sold to Rybolovlev Rothko's *No. 1* for $36 million. During the same year, he sold to Rybolovlev Picasso's *Joueur de Flûte et Femme* Nue for $25 million, having purchased it in Paris for $3,5 million just a day earlier.

By this time, another Freeport, the Asian one in Singapore, had begun to function. Bouvier began building it in 2006. By the end of 2008, most of the structure was finished, but Bouvier planned further development and expansion of the port.

In 2009-2010, Bouvier was still dealing with various procedural issues: the national parliament of Singapore had to pass the relevant legislation allowing the opening of a Freeport in Singapore. Parliament passed the legislation. The project cost Bouvier around $100 million.

As in the world of high art, the world of big business is cloaked with mystery. The seller, the buyer, and their partners never reveal their cards under the guise of commercial or trade secrecy—or at least try not to reveal them. Those clients who visited Bouvier's storage facilities in Freeports in Geneva, Luxembourg, and Singapore were impressed by the degree of organization and order exhibited by the Swiss businessman. At the same time, they were suspicious of the facilities' luxuriousness. As written in *The New Yorker* in an article titled "The Bouvier Affair" by Sam Knight,

A Freeport offers few tax advantages and scarcely any security features that a standard bonded warehouse cannot provide. But Bouvier's development in Singapore carried within it two ideas. The first is that Freeports will become hubs in the sixty-billion-dollar international art market, destinations in themselves—places for scholars, restorers, insurers, art-finance specialists, consultants, and dealers. The second idea is that the ultra-rich don't want just another warehouse. 'If you buy a painting for a hundred million, what do you want? You want to feel well,' Bouvier said. 'Why else do people travel in first class?'

In Singapore, Bouvier specified each component, from the fire-resistant walls, coiled through with steel, to the height of the doors: three meters, to admit the largest contemporary installations. 'I chose everything," he said. "The door handles. I'm obsessive about that.' He used a lighting artist named Johanna Grawunder, whose work he collects, and commissioned an enormous sculpture, La Cage sans Frontières, by the Israeli artist and designer Ron Arad, to stand in the atrium.

The opening of the Singapore Freeport, and its immediate success—Christie's took a space—brought Bouvier international attention. The facilities tapped into a fascination with the tastes and financial shenanigans of the one percent. [...] Bouvier's rivals in the art-logistics trade watched, fascinated and somewhat bemused. Art shippers are unshowy folks. They didn't understand why Bouvier and Natural Le Coultre were making such a fuss over their warehouses. One rival, who visited the Singapore Freeport and saw the Arad in the atrium, told me, "If a client of mine walked into my office and saw a five-million-dollar sculpture, he would assume I was charging him too much.' Others couldn't work out where Bouvier was getting the money. Natural Le Coultre's profits had historically been a few million dollars a year. 'Of course, we wondered,' one told me. 'We are not billionaires. And to build Freeports you need to be a billionaire'."[47]

It was in the Singapore Freeport that Bouvier hid most of Rybolovlev's masterpieces, saving them from Elena's lawyers and bailiffs: four paintings by Modigliani, two by Monet, Van Gogh, Gauguin, two by Picasso, Degas, and Rothko. He sent the heavy and large works of art, plus one Picasso and one Modigliani, to London, where by that time there were already many rich Russians whose identities and capitals were protected by British justice from encroachment by the Russian authorities and law enforcement agencies, and all this was sent to Singapore and London before 22 December 2008, i.e. before Elena Rybolovleva filed for divorce. In particular, by the time Rybolovleva filed a petition on 29 December 2008 to temporarily seize Rybolovlev's assets worldwide, Rybolovlev's masterpieces were no longer in Switzerland and Monaco.

Part of the collection, however, was kept in Cyprus. Bouvier did not create a Freeport there. Rybolovlev himself built a Freeport in Cyprus, making the entire Greek part of the island of Cyprus a Freeport for himself.

5

How Much Does Cyprus Cost?

Rybolovlev created difficulties with his divorce with his own hands, because he did not want to share the money. However, the sums were large. Initially, the spouses agreed that only the money lying in the account of one of the trusts in the amount of approximately $2 billion would be considered jointly acquired money. Accordingly, Elena Rybolovleva was to receive part of this money, which in the presence of a Swiss judge divorcing Rybolovleva agreed to. They were given a month to sign the final papers. But when Rybolovlev appeared before the judge a month later, he suddenly stated that he personally, as promised, was ready to pay Elena her share, but the trust refused to pay such money and asked for a reduction.

Rybolovlev, indeed, by this time had no phone, no accounts, no credit cards, no assets recorded on him. Everything was in a trust. On paper, he personally owned nothing at all, and in the courts, he testified either as a witness or as a consultant to one of his trusts. But the judge, who had seen a lot in her life, understood that the trust was Rybolovlev, and therefore in July 2010 ordered Rybolovlev to pay his ex-wife $4,5 billion—half of Rybolovlev's total fortune, estimated "as everyone knows" at $9 billion. The judge wanted to force the parties to return to the previously reached agreement on the old terms, and the revision of the decision was nothing more than a way to put pressure on Rybolovlev.

Now it was time for Rybolovlev to panic, and instead of going back to the old original agreement, he started looking for ways to circumvent the Swiss court's decision.

In September 2010, Rybolovlev bought a 9,7% stake in the Bank of

Cyprus for $500 million. There is no doubt that this was done with consent and in Russia's strategic interests, which included control of the Cypriot economy and political life of the island for Russia's takeover of the Cypriot bridgehead in the European Union.

The Russian infiltration into Cyprus and taking control of the Bank of Cyprus is a detective and spy story worthy of Le Carré's pen. The bank's largest shareholder was the Cypriot government, which owned 18% of the bank through the People's Bank of Cyprus. But by 2013, six of the 16 members of the Bank of Cyprus' board of directors were Russian citizens.

Together with the share of the leading Cypriot bank, Rybolovlev gradually found himself with the entire leadership of the island in his pocket. Acquiring a stake in the bank also allowed Rybolovlev to influence the country's financial and trust laws. At his request, law firm Andreas Neocleous drafted an amendment to the 1992 trust law that included a clause granting the right not to disclose the identity of the ultimate beneficial owner of the trust (which violated the relevant anti-money laundering regulation of the European Union, of which Cyprus was a member). In October 2010, just three months after the publication of Elena Rybolovleva's financial claims in the divorce case, Maria Kyriacou, MP for The Democratic Rally (DISY) and partner at law firm Andreas Neocleous, introduced the bill in Parliament. Easily dubbed the "Rybolovlev's Law" by a French journalist covering the event, the bill was aimed at preventing Elena Rybolovleva from finding her husband's accounts and assets.

To overcome the contradiction between the "Rybolovleva Law" and European law, a clause was included in the amendment, according to which all foreign court judgments were to be considered "as contrary to public order in the Republic and therefore inapplicable in Cyprus". With this amendment, if Rybolovlev's wife won a court judgment in Switzerland ordering her ex-husband to transfer to her part of his property registered in an international trust in Cyprus, the judgment would become inapplicable and the case would have to be retried in Cyprus on "public order" grounds.

Supporters of the law in Parliament argued that it would encourage more investment in Cyprus, including from Russia, citing Rybolovlev's investments in the Bank of Cyprus. On 8 March 2012, the law was passed by Parliament almost unanimously (only two MPs voted against the amendment). Immediately afterward, a resolution was passed to increase the authorized capital of the Bank of Cyprus. But Rybolovlev refused to increase his capital in the bank, thus breaking his promise to invest in Cyprus.

Instead, he started to finance the presidential campaign of Nicos Anastasiades and put his private jet at his disposal for the period of elections. This was important for Anastasiades, as the private plane at Anastasiades' disposal was his weakness, his favorite toy.

Anastasiades made a deal with Rybolovlev to fund his election campaign in exchange for helping him divorce his wife back in 2012. Elena Rybolovlev claimed half of their $9 billion fortune, most of which Rybolovlev had stashed away in trusts in Cyprus managed by Neocleus. Anastasiades promised Rybolovlev that if elected president he would protect his fortune. The mediator in this agreement was Andreas Neocleus, Rybolovlev's representative in Cyprus. From then on Anastasiades was loyal to Rybolovlev and could not back down.

Anastasiades won and became president. "I brought Anastasiades to where he is now, without me he would not be there,"—repeatedly and to various acquaintances Rybolovlev repeated, specifying that Anastasiades "personally promised me that he would deal with my wife's case" and that he, Rybolovlev, "controls the president of Cyprus."[48]

However, Rybolovlev was not the only and most likely not the main Russian donor putting Nicos Anastasiades as "his" president in Cyprus. The second was Vladimir Strzhalkovsky.

Strzhalkovsky was an unremarkable man. He was a vice president of the Bank of Cyprus and a close associate of Putin's in the state security line. Of course, he was KGB/FSB. In addition to Cyprus, he was also in charge of Africa, especially South Africa, for the FSB. In 2012, he became famous for his resignation as CEO of Norilsk Nickel (he gave up his position to Vladimir Potanin, but remained the company's vice-president in charge of the development of foreign divisions) after negotiations with Putin and Prime Minister Dmitry Medvedev, he received a $100 million compensation for his resignation. Speaking at a press conference in Moscow to mark the extraordinary event, Strzhalkovsky said he would donate 10% of his bonus to a charity that helps widows and orphans of FSB officers. $50 million of the remaining $90 million was placed in Bank of Cyprus and the rest was converted into shares in the bank. Strzhalkovsky allegedly owned 0,66% of

Bank of Cyprus shares, which corresponded to deposits of more than €60 million. The person who brought Strzhalkovsky's cash from Moscow to Cyprus was the future president of Cyprus, Nicos Anastasiades. Strzhalkovsky was at the same time also a client of Anastasiades' law firm, which allowed both to maintain an open business relationship.

This is what Makarios Drousiotis, special adviser to President Anastasiades, writes in his yet unpublished book[49] on corruption and Russian infiltration of Cyprus about Anastasiades (who had just won the 2013 presidential election) and Strzhalkovsky:

> With the ceremonials out of the way and Anastasiades' election as the seventh President of the Republic of Cyprus a formality, a motorcade was put together to escort the new president to his campaign HQ and later to the 'Eleftheria' indoor stadium where he was to give his victory speech. Last in the convoy was a black armored car transporting the Russian guest. I later found out that Anastasiades' guest was Vladimir Strzhalkovsky.
>
> When in September 2013 it became known that of the 16 members of the new Bank of Cyprus board six of them were Russians, the international media focused on Strzhalkovsky because of his resume—a former KGB agent and a Putin man. At the time I recalled a discussion I had had with Anastasiades in his office, in 2012. I was getting ready to travel to the United States to do some research on public records for a book I was writing on Soviet policy on the Cyprus issue… So, during this talk, he asked me how I was going to pay for my trip to America. "I have money," I replied. He then asked if I needed more. I said no. In case the reason I had declined was that I felt I would be burdening him, he assured me he had collected a great deal of money for the election campaign… Besides, he added, he had received unlimited funds for his election campaign from contributions by Russian friends of his… Anastasiades specifically referred to one particular Russian, whose name slipped my mind at the time and who, as Anastasiades told me, owned nickel mines in Siberia and was a friend of Vladimir Putin's. I later discovered that Anastasiades' friend and funder was Vladimir Strzhalkovsky.
>
> Like Putin, Strzhalkovsky comes from Leningrad, and they served

together in the KGB. With the collapse of the Soviet Union Strzhalkovsky entered the private sector and set up Neva travel agency. In the 1990s the Neva travel agency took part in a bus tour from Saint Petersburg to the Finnish city of Kotka. Young Russian women were being bused to motels/brothels. Because of this affair… Strzhalkovsky came to be known as "the KGB's pimp".

When Putin came to power in 1999, Strzhalkovsky took on several important government positions, including that of Deputy Finance Minister and Deputy Minister of Tourism… In 2008 Putin put him in charge of rescuing Norilsk Nickel, which was in the throes of a drawn-out dispute between two oligarchs, who were its major shareholders—Vladimir Potanin and Oleg Deripaska. Both had companies in Cyprus through which they managed their businesses in Russia. With Putin's blessing, Strzhalkovsky was appointed chairman of Norilsk Nickel. Putin personally paid a visit to the company's mines and met with Strzhalkovsky in his office to get briefed on the status of the company. As executive chairman of Norilsk Nickel, Strzhalkovsky undertook a special mission as a mediator between Putin and the then-president of South Africa, Jacob Zuma.

Towards the end of March 2011, a private plane landed at South Africa's King Shaka International Airport. It had come from Russia and was carrying medical equipment for a mobile diagnostic lab, a donation from a company called Norilsk Nickel to the Nkandla community, from where the then president of South Africa, Jacob Zuma originated. Norilsk Nickel is a huge Russian mining and smelting company, which had invested in South African mines. The dispatch had been organized by Vladimir Strzhalkovsky

Zuma rose through the ranks of the African National Congress during the time of apartheid. He was in charge of the information sector. At the time Strzhalkovsky was a KGB agent, active on the African continent. As a close associate of Russian President, Vladimir Putin, he used his contacts with African liberation movements to promote Russian interests in Africa. Strzhalkovsky took part in the handing over ceremony of the medical donation and then had a meeting with Zuma. Three months later, Zuma visited Sochi where he signed a strategic cooperation agreement between Russia and South Africa.

During his visit to Sochi, Zuma met again with Strzhalkovsky.

In 2013 Putin appointed Strzhalkovsky as Rosatom's special envoy to promote nuclear energy in African countries. In August 2014 Zuma visited Russia and had lengthy private discussions with Putin. A few weeks later a secret agreement on nuclear cooperation was signed between Russia and South Africa. The agreement provided for the construction of a nuclear power plant in South Africa to the tune of 78 billion dollars and would be the largest project ever built in South Africa.

Throughout his presidency, Zuma proved to be one of the most pro-Russian leaders in the world. He visited Russia many times and often spoke with Putin over the phone. In 2018 Zuma was forced to step down by his party, as a result of his involvement in numerous very serious corruption cases, which included the nuclear cooperation agreement with Russia, a project that was abandoned after his resignation... The nuclear agreement between Russia and South Africa... his appointment as special envoy to Africa of Rosatom and his secret agreement on the huge contract of $78 billion, all stemmed from his relationship with Putin...

When Strzhalkovsky singled out Anastasiades to represent his interests, he didn't pick him at random from the Yellow Pages. Anastasiades was a politically exposed person and front-runner to win the next elections, therefore a target for corruption to control the political game in Cyprus. In this world of underground relationships and secret deals, where kickbacks are transferred in cash by private jet, business is not upfront. The money that Anastasiades was handling for Strzhalkovsky was dirty money and nobody knew how much of it actually belonged to Strzhalkovsky, how much belonged to Putin, and how much belonged to the KGB.

...In June 2012, in a bid to avert impending default, the government of Demetris Christofias had been forced to resort to the European Financial Stability Mechanism. The solutions on the table were tough, and talks with the Troika of future lenders (European Commission, European Central Bank, and International Monetary Fund) reached an impasse... In no uncertain terms, the Troika let it be known that the Russians must not be allowed to control the new board at Bank of Cyprus. And so began the wheeling and dealing over who would sit on the board, so that the Russians would not hold the majority. Averof Neophytou [deputy chairman of the DISY party] considered to be the "master of wheeling and dealing," held talks with the political parties, the archbishop, bank employee unions, and, of course, the five law firms representing the major Russian depositors.

"Major Russian depositors" essentially already owned Cyprus. The situation had been set in motion; positions irreversibly surrendered. In his book Diary of the Eurocrisis in Cyprus, former Central Bank of Cyprus Governor Panicos Demetriades writes that Cypriot law firms with close ties to banks and local politics actively solicited Russian depositors, to whom they offered protection from potential audits. Jeroen Dijsselbloem, Eurogroup President during the Cyprus financial crisis, shares this opinion: "There was a tight-knit network of lawyers working in financial services who also engaged in politics. The connection was also visible between the banks and politics, and was among others the cause for the deep problems facing Cyprus." Anastasiades was at the center of this coterie, as he combined the dual capacities of lawyer and politician and had, according to Dijsselbloem, "considerable skill attracting wealthy Russian clients." Makarios Drousiotis writes:

> The largest influx of Russian deposits into Cyprus occurred between 2004 and 2010. With Cyprus having joined the EU, Russian oligarchs saw Cyprus as a safe destination for their money. Many of these deposits were laundered here and then funneled back to Russia as European investments, safe from confiscation by the regime. During this timeframe, the banking sector in Cyprus doubled in size, accounting for 953% of GDP."
>
> Russian money was deposited into accounts held by shell companies. Shells conduct no business, but are legal entities that safeguard the identities of their true owners... Other than raking in introducer fees, law firms also charged for transactions conducted on behalf of their clients, making a killing... Law firms with mediocre business grew into gigantic outfits, with swanky offices, while the partners turned millionaires in the blink of an eye. The Nicos Chr. Anastasiades & Partners law firm was among these parvenus...

During the golden decade of banking in Cyprus, Anastasiades amassed a total of more than €10 million from the Bank of Cyprus, which was channeled tax-free abroad. If this income was legal and ethical, it should have been invoiced in Cyprus, VAT paid and income tax paid. By depositing them abroad, it remained invisible and tax-free.

Bankers granted foreign depositors exorbitantly high-interest rates, in some cases reaching 10% for five years. To manage this warped state of affairs, the banks began making risky investments, expanding their operations overseas into unknown and high-risk markets like Russia, Ukraine, and other former eastern bloc countries.

Negotiations to appoint a new Bank of Cyprus board of directors in 2013 culminated in what Panicos Demetriades in his book calls the Averof List. Demetriades intended to subject Strzhalkovsky and other Russian candidates to rigorous vetting. Some candidates on the Averof List did not even submit their CVs to the Central Bank of Cyprus following the formal standard procedure. These included Strzhalkovsky. According to Demetriades, the Central Bank staff conducting the vetting knew nothing about Strzhalkovsky's background other than information published in the Financial Times that he was a friend of Putin and a former KGB officer. It was assumed that he was unlikely to be approved to work at the bank.

Anastasiades, having learned of Demetriades' intention to reject Russian candidates, especially Strzhalkovsky, called the Central Bank governor and told him the following: "I hope you won't reject the candidates to be nominated by the Resolution Authority, as they will be elected for certain." Demetriades replied that he had already endorsed ten people on the list but could not form an opinion on the other six, Russians, because they had not yet filled in the relevant forms with their data. "I'm the master hustler of politics." Anastasiades replied. "No one has ever hustled me, nor will you. Not only am I the best hustler, I'm also the biggest pimp out there... "Panicos dear, I'd like to thank you in advance." Saying this, he hung up.

That same day the new board of directors of the bank was approved. It included all six Russian representatives. Strzhalkovsky was elected vice-chairman.

In 2014, Wilbur Ross, future US Secretary of Commerce in Trump's Cabinet, invested €400 million into the Bank of Cyprus and became, along with Strzhalkovsky, its vice president and deputy chairman. One of Ross's first decisions as vice chairman was to promote Joseph Ackermann, a former Deutsche Bank Chief Executive, a Chairman of the Bank of Cyprus. Ackermann had close ties to Russia and a good relationship with Putin and Herman Gref, the chief executive of Sberbank. Sberbank was under US and EU sanctions those days because of the Russian annexation of Crimea.

In 2015 the Russian business of Bank of Cyprus was sold to Russian banker Artem Avetisyan for €7 million. Avetisyan who also was working for the Sberbank purchased a stake in Bank of Cyprus in 2008 for €450 million. The London office of Deutsche Bank advised that deal.

Deutsche Bank, for many years, was Trump's main creditor. At the same time, Deutsche Bank was involved in a money laundering operation through the banks in Cyprus, Estonia, and Latvia related to the $10 billion of Russian money and had to pay a $630 million fine to the State of New York in January 2017, after Trump already won the Presidential Election[50].

Anastasiades remained president of Cyprus until 28 February 2023[51]. Throughout these years, he repeatedly used Rybolovlev who provided him his own, or a rented private jet paid for by Rybolovlev[52].

In the autumn of 2013, Rybolovlev's lawyers, without any opposition from the defense of Elena Rybolovleva, who was absent in Cyprus, embarked on plans that cannot be described as anything other than an abuse of justice. Using the Rybolovlev Law, Rybolovlev's Aries trust to which some of Rybolovleva's assets were registered, asked Judge Harris Solomonidis at the District Court of Nicosia for an injunction against any action by Elena Rybolovleva and her lawyers against Rybolovlev's trusts anywhere in the world. On 9 October 2013, Solomonidis signed a temporary injunction prohibiting Rybolovleva and her lawyers to take "any legal proceedings in any court other than the Cypriot courts.... in support of her alleged rights arising out of her matrimonial relationship with her husband."

On 20 January 2014, Solomonidis issued another order barring nine of Rybolovleva's lawyers in Switzerland, the US and the UK from pursuing legal claims against Rybolovleva's trusts. In other words, Elena was prohibited from bringing any proceedings against her ex-husband's trusts anywhere in the world except Cyprus.

Immediately after the second injunction was granted in favor of

Rybolovlev, the judge's wife was employed by A. Neocleous Trust Company Ltd. On 13 May 2014, Rybolovleva's Cypriot lawyer Alexandra Pelayia filed a motion to disqualify the judge on the grounds of bias, as both applications for injunctions were deliberately made to the same judge. However, the motion was denied. Judge Solomonidis himself considered the motion for recusal and dismissed it. In his ruling, he stated that both applications had been submitted to him "according to the current case schedule being followed by the court registrar" and that his wife's subsequent employment with Neocleous was not a basis for his recusal. In July 2014, he converted both injunctions from temporary to permanent. This removed Rybolovleva's ability to initiate legal action against Cypriot trusts anywhere in the world other than Cyprus.

Since under the new law property held in Cyprus could only be subject to division in Cyprus and in a Cypriot court, Rybolovlev invited Elena to Cyprus to divide the artworks held in Cyprus in a specially equipped air-conditioned room in the basement of Neocleous' Limassol office. Now, in Bouvier's presence, the Rybolovlevs will have to agree in a civilized manner on who keeps which paintings.

However, Rybolovlev's real intentions were quite different. Using his unlimited influence in Cyprus, he planned to arrest his wife on charges of stealing a diamond ring from him and force her in prison to sign divorce papers on his terms.

At the time of the divorce, the diamond ring, worth around €25 million, was the only significant asset Elena owned. It was a gift from her husband on her 40th birthday. All the rest of the money was in various kinds of trusts. Elena planned to either sell the ring or use it as collateral to borrow money against it to finance the divorce proceedings. Technically, the ring was registered to the family Domus Trust. But it was registered to the trust much later, in connection with Rybolovlev's planned divorce. Elena didn't even know about it.

Arresting a foreign citizen in Cyprus for "theft" committed in another country was not easy either. Cypriot laws did not provide for such a possibility. Then the resourceful Rybolovlev came up with the idea of amending the Criminal Code of Cyprus. On 9 October 2013, the same day that the injunction proceedings against Elena and her lawyers began, Rybolovlev's new lawyer Averof Neophytou[53], who had been lured by him from his opponents, submitted another "Rybolovlev Law" to the House of Representatives Legal Affairs Committee to amend the Criminal Code. On 23 October, after only 15 days (as opposed to the 15 months it took to pass the Rybolovlev Law), Parliament unanimously passed the amendment "to bolster and enhance Cyprus as an international business center."

Under the amendment, the jurisdiction of the Cypriot courts was extended to "adjudicate on offenses committed in any foreign country by any natural person, if the offense caused damage or injury to property or denied or retained property outside the Republic which directly or indirectly belongs.. to a corporation with a registered office in the Republic or to a trust governed by Cypriot law". For example, the Rybolovlev trust to which his ex-wife's diamond ring was transferred.

In other words, under the amendment, the alleged theft of a jewelry item in Switzerland by a permanent resident of Switzerland became a criminal offense in Cyprus if the item was stolen from a trust registered in the Republic of Cyprus. However, since the alleged "theft" of the ring took place in Switzerland in 2009, the law provided for a penalty for retaining the "stolen" property of the trust. Rybolovleva was supposed to be tried for "stealing" the ring in 2009 and keeping it in her possession ever since, well after Cyprus passed a 2013 amendment to its penal code making it an offense to keep "stolen" property.

Senior Cypriot officials, including the President, were aware of, or directly involved in, the impending operation to arrest Rybolovleva in Cyprus. President personal public relations adviser Andreas Hadjikiriakos coordinated the arrest[54]. Deputy Attorney General Rikkos Erotokritou, who was in direct contact with Rybolovlev, was also involved in the operation.

In December 2013, Sergei Chernitsyn, an employee of Rybolovlev's family office, traveled to Cyprus to coordinate with local authorities this operation. Chernitsyn scheduled a meeting with Justice Minister Ionas Nicolaou for 11 December 2013. Whether this meeting took place or not is not entirely clear (Nicolaou himself claimed later that he did not meet with anyone). However, the Ministry of Justice and Nicolaou personally were actively involved in the operation to arrest Elena.

On 7 February, a teleconference took place between Rybolovlev and the well-known Cypriot lawyer Leandros Papaphilippou, whom Rybolovlev planned to hire to join his team of lawyers. Despite much persuasion,

Papaphilippou refused.

On 13 February, Rybolovlev arrived in Cyprus with Bersheda to agree on a plan of action with Andreas Neocleous and Hadjikiriakos. Final amendments were made to the plan. Elena was to be lured to Cyprus on 24 February and arrested right at Larnaca airport.

At Neocleous' law firm, the issue of Rybolovlev's arrest was handled by Andreas Neocleous' son, lawyer Panayiotis. As soon as the day of Rybolovleva's arrival in Cyprus was determined, Panayiotis, on behalf of the Domus Trust, to which the ring was registered, filed a claim with the Limassol Criminal Investigation Department for the theft of a valuable diamond ring worth €25 million. The statement said that Elena borrowed the ring in 2009 and did not return it. At the same time, an application was prepared against Rybolovleva to the MOKAS anti-money laundering unit for the alleged laundering of money derived from the sale or pledge of the ring.

The operation was coordinated by Bersheda, who coordinated all necessary matters with Andreas Neocleous and Rybolovleva's other Cypriot lawyers. In particular, Bersheda informed the lawyers of Rybolovleva's passport number and the time her plane would land at the airport: "The passport number …73, issued on 4 June 2013. They should land around noon—1 pm but I'll text you the exact time later," she wrote in one of her texts forwarded to Rybolovlev's Cypriot lawyers.

By Sunday 23 February 2014, an arrest warrant for Elena had not yet been issued. Bersheda, who had coordinated the preparation of the arrest, wrote a text to Panayiotis Neocleous that day asking for updates on the situation with the warrant. Panayiotis replied, 'Just spoke with the policeman. The aw [arrest warrant] will be applied for within the next two hours. Let us keep our fingers crossed." Indeed, on Sunday, Andreas Neocleous finally got the warrant signed by Deputy Attorney General Erotokritou.

On the same day, Andreas Hadjikiriakos informed Sergei Chernitsyn of the results of his communication with Justice Minister Nicolaou: 'I confirmed it with MoJ [Ministry of Justice] that she will be put on the stop list tomorrow and will be arrested at passport control in the private lounge. This is the legal procedure when there is a warrant."

Although the arrest warrant was technically legal, everything that happened was a well-organized provocation and trap, from the amendments to the Penal Code urgently passed by the Cypriot Parliament to the coordination of the arrest between the police and Rybolovlev's lawyers. It was difficult to consider this conspiracy against Rybolovleva as legal.

Elena, together with Bouvier, flew to Cyprus on a private jet chartered by Bouvier as planned—on 24 February 2014, at 7.45 a.m. Geneva time. She planned to return to Switzerland the same day, along with the selected paintings. At 11.15 am Cyprus time (10.15 am Geneva time), Bersheda sends a text to Panayiotis Neocleous: "Any news? Managed to reach N?" "N", aka "NA", aka "N1" is none other than the President of Cyprus, Nicos Anastasiades. Panayiotis replied, 'He is in a meeting with 15 people. He will call as soon as he finishes."

The president was indeed meeting at that moment with a delegation from the Association of National Organization of Cypriot Fighters. But immediately after the end of that meeting, he had a word with Andreas Neocleous and was briefed on the progress of the operation to detain Rybolovleva. "N1 is informed," Chernitsyn reported to Bersheda after his conversation with Andreas Neocleous. "AN [Andreas Neocleous] talked with N1. The reaction is good. N1 said that "he hopes" that AG [attorney-general] will not interfere.

The arrest warrant was signed by the deputy attorney general, and Attorney General Costas Clerides had the authority to cancel it.

The plane landed at Larnaca airport at around 1.30 pm. Two criminal investigation officers waited for Elena at the Skylink private jet terminal and immediately arrested her. Rybolovleva asked to speak to her lawyers, was authorized to do so, and contacted them. While waiting for the lawyers from Nicosia, police officers held Rybolovleva for about an hour in a room inside the airport terminal. Also in the terminal was Chernitsyn, who kept informing Bersheda by texts of what was happening: "She is still at the airport. Waiting for her lawyer," he wrote in one of the texts.

The delay at the airport awaiting the arrival of Rybolovleva's lawyers and the possible intervention of the Cypriot attorney general could have disrupted the operation. Bersheda contacted Leandros Papaphilippou again and asked for his cooperation, perhaps so that he could intercede with the attorney general if necessary. Papaphilippou again replied with a refusal, citing busyness.

At around 3 pm, Chernitsyn informed Bersheda that Rybolovleva was traveling to Limassol in a police car. She was followed by the Mercedes of Alexandra Pelayia, Rybolovleva's lawyer, with three colleagues. At 3.36 pm, Chernitsyn sent a text that Rybolovleva had arrived at Limassol police station. The interrogation began. Elena told police that the ring was given to her by her husband in 2008, that it was specially made to fit her finger and belonged to her, that the Domus Trust was registered two years later, in 2010, and that she was not aware that the ring belonged to the trust.

"She is saying to the police that it [the ring] was a gift," Chernitsyn reported to Bersheda an hour after the questioning began.

The next day, an invoice for the purchase of the ring, drawn up in Elena's name and signed by English jeweler Lawrence Graff, was flown from Geneva to Cyprus and handed over to police authorities. As Tania Rappo told in one of her interviews, she happened to witness Rybolovlev buying and giving the ring to his wife. It was Rappo who suggested that Elena's name be put on the invoice to obtain insurance for the expensive purchase.

Shortly after Rybolovleva's arrest, the legal firm Neocleous, acting as trustee of the trust, rushed to announce her arrest. Andreas Neocleous said in a statement that the ring theft charge had nothing to do with Dmitry Rybolovlev and the trustees' only concern was protecting the trust's assets.

News of Rybolovleva's arrest became an international sensation. But when Rybolovlev was asked if he felt sorry to keep the mother of his children in jail, he said that Elena was not worth the billions (over which there was a dispute at the time). "There are three places in the world where I can do whatever I want: Skorpios, Cyprus, and Monaco. I'm certainly not going to pay $4 billion... Let Elena know she's not getting anything. I have done everything I had to do in Cyprus for this," Rybolovlev said.

The case was turning into a farce as there was no real evidence of a crime committed by Rybolovleva. Rybolovleva was able to show investigators a copy of the invoice with her name on it, the announcement of the arrest, made in self-promotion by people involved in the operation, attracted unnecessary international media attention. Limassol police chief Andreas Koushioumis refused to consent to Rybolovleva's continued detention. She was released seven hours after being detained, although police took her passport from her. 'She left the docs and is leaving the police station now", reported Chernitsyn, who was at the police station with Panayiotis Neokleous at the time.

Rybolovleva returned to Nicosia with Pelayia, at whose house she stayed overnight. She appealed to the Russian embassy for protection. She was given an appointment to meet with the ambassador the next day, Tuesday 25 February, in the morning. The Russian Embassy offered Rybolovleva protection and she spent the following night in the Embassy building.

On the same day, 25 February, Pelayia visited Attorney General Costas Clerides and told him what had happened. The latter telephoned Limassol Criminal Investigation Chief Yiannis Soteriadis and ordered that any questions regarding the Rybolovleva case should be addressed directly to him. The plan to arrest and detain Rybolovleva completely failed.

However, on the day of Elena's arrest at Larnaca airport, a contempt of court application was filed by Rybolovlev against her and her lawyers in a Cypriot court. The new case was based on the "Rybolovlev Law" and orders from the Nicosia court to cease any future litigation against Cypriot trusts abroad. The court application was due to be heard in a month, and Rybolovlev's lawyers planned to serve Elena with a summons while she was in Cyprus, in the hope of keeping her in Cyprus for a month until the case was decided.

On Wednesday, 26 February, Rybolovleva was again summoned to Limassol's criminal investigation department under the pretext of giving additional testimony. Rybolovlev's lawyers planned to serve her there with a summons to appear in court for a contempt of court hearing. After spotting a man outside the courthouse who usually serves subpoenas and lawyers from the Neocleous law firm, Rybolovleva headed to the bathroom, where she swapped coats and black glasses with one of her lawyers of similar build. Pelayia has so far called the Attorney General's Office and demanded that the police return the passport.

When the cross-dressing hoax was discovered, Rybolovleva was already rushing, lying flat on the back of her car, to Larnaca airport to leave Cyprus as soon as possible. She was accompanied by Pelayia to make sure that nothing happened to Rybolovleva on the way. The nearest flight was to London. The epic with the arrest in Cyprus was over. Elena never returned to Cyprus again. According to the lawyer Papaphilippou, the operation to arrest Elena cost Rybolovlev at least €20 million.

"If she had spent a few weeks in jail, she would have signed any documents I wanted" to get out, Rybolovlev told Tania Rappo a few weeks later, referring to his ex-wife's arrest in Cyprus. But his ex-wife was no longer there[55].

6

Buying the Salvator Mundi and Breaking Up with Bouvier

Bouvier traveled back from Cyprus alone. He could have broken off his relationship with Rybolovlev already then, in 2014, but the price of such a breakup was too high. When I asked Bouvier in 2019 what he would have changed in his life if he had known how his epic relationship with Rybolovlev would end, Bouvier replied, "I would have left him five years ago, full stop."

While already in Switzerland, Elena published a letter she wrote to the attorney general of Geneva that her ex-husband Dmitry should be the first on the list of suspects in case of her death, and later managed to seize her ex-husband's assets around the world. However, Rybolovlev succeeded in getting the seizure lifted from his assets in Singapore and London.

The seizure of Rybolovlev's Swiss assets remained in force, but Rybolovlev's masterpieces were no longer stored there. The prudent Bouvier moved everything out in advance.

Bouvier took a very active part in lifting the arrest from Rybolovlev's masterpieces in Singapore and London. He signed an affidavit stating that the paintings were bought from him by Rybolovlev, that he participated in the selection and registration of payments for the paintings personally and without his wife, and that these objects of art were not part of joint ownership[56].

While Bouvier was drawing up that affidavit at the notary's office in Geneva, Rybolovlev, like a delinquent child, was waiting for him outside the notary's office. And when Bouvier finally came out, for the first and last time in his life Bouvier heard Rybolovlev say "thank you".

Nothing out of the ordinary Bouvier had done. He would likely have provided similar assistance to any of his major clients. Bouvier was asked to safely hide the paintings and not to inform Rybolovlev's wife about the new purchases. But there was nothing illegal in all this, and Bouvier's status in the eyes of Rybolovlev changed. He became part of Rybolovlev's inner circle. He began to be invited to birthday parties, which usually had very few people, only the closest people, 5-6 people at most, mostly those who had worked with Rybolovlev back in Uralkali.

Rybolovlev was an extremely boring person who had no friends. He didn't drink because it was important for him to be in control of himself. He never would show his emotions. Even when his team won a game, judging by his face, one might think that his team had lost. He would show emotion for about three seconds when a goal was scored (unless for PR reasons it was necessary to rejoice for extra time so that photographers could capture a happy Rybolovlev hugging in the stadium with the Prince of Monaco). Even on his birthday, he was always sad.

He didn't know how to have fun. He lived by a strict schedule: he got up at 7 a.m., and then everything was scheduled—what time was breakfast, what was for breakfast, what time was lunch, what was for lunch... In the evening, most of the time, he was walking around his office in circles and went to bed early.

"I met many oligarchs in Russia," Bouvier recounted. "But these were people who were to be able to have fun, to be able to relax. Whoever they were, they had that human element of being able to have fun. Rybolovlev was always a very flat person, very monotonous. He didn't become an oligarch thanks to his lack of charm and charisma."

Yet, while he was a boring client, he was also a very important client. To buy new paintings, Rybolovlev registered a new company, unrelated to the first one, and bought art confidentially without informing Elena. Even Sazonov, Rybolovlev's closest employee, was now unaware of what was being bought and did not handle the paperwork for the purchases as he had done previously. The paperwork went through a separate, also new, company created by Rybolovlev called Rybolovlev Monaco, and all the masterpieces bought were sent to Singapore without even passing through Switzerland because of Dmitry's divorce proceedings with Elena.

After learning that Rybolovlev was fond of nude models by Modigliani,

Bouvier in 2006 managed to obtain the canvas *Lying Nude with Arms Raised* (for $26,7 million), and in November 2011, through an intermediary managed to persuade the famous New York financier Steven Cohen to remove from the wall and sell (it was hanging in the dining room) Modigliani's painting *Nude on a Blue Cushion (Nu Couché au Coussin Bleu)* for $93,5 million. He resold it to Rybolovlev for $118 million.

In February 2013, Bouvier sold to Rybolovlev a piece by Toulouse-Lautrec for €14 million. During the same year, he managed to procure for $123 million Gustav Klimt's masterpiece *Wasserschlangen II* and to resell it to Rybolovlev for $183 million; Paul Gaugin's *Otahi* and *Te Fare (La Maison)* (1892), which Rybolovlev bought for $120 million and $85 million, respectively; Auguste Rodin's sculptures *L'Eternel Printemps* and *Le Baiser Grand Modele* (a 2010 copy of the 1880s original), which Rybolovlev paid $48,1 million and $10,4 million, respectively; Rene Magritte's *Le domaine d'Arnheim* (1938), which Rybolovlev bought for $43,5 million; and, finally, Leonardo da Vinci's *Salvator Mundi*, accidentally found and miraculously preserved, which was purchased by Bouvier for approximately $80 million and resold by him to Rybolovlev for $127,5 million.

Rybolovlev first saw *Salvator Mundi* in a photograph, and not from Bouvier, and was ready to buy it immediately, offering the intermediary selling the painting $190 million.

—You want to buy *Salvator Mundi,* Bouvier asked when he came to see Rybolovlev.—Keep in mind that no one is fighting over this purchase.

—Yes, I like that painting very much, Rybolovlev confirmed.

Bouvier then drafted a two-page letter for Rybolovlev, describing all the problems with the painting and urging him not to buy it because the painting had been too much, too long, and too expensive to restore. Here is that letter, sent on 22 March 2013 to Sazonov for Rybolovlev in French and Russian:

> *Analyses:*
> Salvator Mundi
> Leonardo Da Vinci
> Painting on walnut wood boards
> 65,6 x 45,4.
> Late 1490 or early 1500.

Subject:

Christ holding a transparent globe in his hand.

The work was found in very poor condition, provenance Coll. Cook. Restored and authenticated.

The conservation condition is fragile, the face is almost invisible, and only the hand and the lapel of the sleeve appear to be authentic.

My first analysis:

The people who are interested in this painting—Warren Adelson (an American art dealer from New York) and Robin Simon (also an art dealer). They sold part of the painting to one investor.

I don't think Ashton Hawkins is that investor. He has a reputation for being slick and business savvy. He is one of the heads of the Metropolitan Museum of Art and has connections with Christie's. I will try to find out if he is a member of the "consortium" selling this painting.

Leonardo Da Vinci's Salvator Mundi is a very beautiful painting, and I understand people's interest in it. In all likelihood, the painting is his handiwork.

Nevertheless, it has a significant problem:

1) The painting was in badly damaged condition. The hands are the best preserved. Everything else was restored: Diane Modestini did a remarkable restoration job, which she publicly spoke about at the National Gallery;

The painting was restored over five years, which is a long time.

It seems that the restorer Diane Modestini also has an interest in selling this painting.

There is a restoration document, but with photos and a good restorer, it will be possible to show the "scenario" of finding and cleaning the painting.

2) The second important issue, is the high price of the piece ($200 million) considering that a very small part of the painting was originally painted by Da Vinci's hand.

3) The painting has been known on the market since 2010 and anyone can contact its dealers/owners.

4) None of the major museums in England, the USA, Europe, or elsewhere in the world have wanted to purchase this work. The only one

who tried to buy this painting for personal reasons was Max Anderson, director of the Dallas Museum of Art, but he was unable to raise the funds despite the wealth of the trustees.

5) It is not clear why the Vatican, with its financial strength and given the subject matter of the Christ the Redeemer painting, is not interested in purchasing it.

6) As of 2010, neither foundations nor private buyers are interested in the painting because of the above points.

In conclusion:

It is important to keep in mind that acquiring this painting is not a quality investment and never will be. The decision to purchase should be made for one's satisfaction and the sake of beauty. If the painting were 100% authentic, it would be worth twice as much. Then museums and collectors would fight to acquire it. But the price is too high and does not match the condition of the painting.

A buyer who spends too much money on this painting would be considered a "fool" and would become a general laughing stock.

If, despite this, there is still a strong desire to buy the painting, I insist that no one must know that the person concerned is an oligarch.

Strategy:

The sellers know that the painting will be presented to the Russian billionaire this Tuesday; they are confident and expect a lot from this meeting.

For the sake of modesty, and to reduce their confidence, I suggest canceling this meeting and telling them there is no more interest in the painting.

My strategy would be to go back to the museum situation and negotiate the museum kind of negotiations with the trustees, just as I did with the Dallas Museum.

Thus, approach the sellers under the guise of the Pinacotheca and negotiate, voluntarily hiding myself behind the advice of the donors.

And take your time.

MOREOVER, IT IS NECESSARY TO HAVE THE PAINTING ANALYSED AT THE SPECTRAL ANALYSIS LABORATORY IN GENEVA TO KNOW EXACTLY WHAT PROPORTION OF THE WORK HAS BEEN OVERWRITTEN.

If he has a spending problem, since I didn't have to look for the painting, I can do him [Rybolovlev] that favor.

I'm working on a financial analysis right now.

Yves

Bouvier felt that a *spolvero* examination was necessary. *Spolvero* was a technique originating in Italy in which the outline of a drawing was transferred to a canvas, wall, or other surface using a cloth bag filled with dark powder (e.g. charcoal), which was applied to a sketch on paper or parchment glued to a surface (in this case a board). The powder penetrated through the needle-punched holes in the paper and left the outline of the drawing in the form of fine dotted lines. Da Vinci used *spolvero* paint many or even all of his famous paintings: *The Lady with the Ermine, Portrait of Ginevra de Benci, La Belle Ferroñera, and Mona Lisa*. And so, this analysis, which could easily have been done to see if there was this powder on the board, was never done.

However, Bouvier got the impression that Rybolovlev didn't care whether he was buying a real Da Vinci or not.

Passing the intermediary, with whom he was not in a contractual relationship, and therefore had both formal and moral rights to pass him, Bouvier flew to New York and offered the auction Sotheby's to sign a contract with the owner of the painting to sell it through Sotheby's for $63 million. "Borrowing" the painting from Sotheby's for a $63 million security deposit, he then went to see Rybolovlev. He had the relatively small Da Vinci board with him in an unassuming black bag.

—Do you like this painting?—asked Bouvier when he reached Rybolovlev, taking the Da Vinci out of the bag and placing the board in front of Rybolovlev on a chair.

The deal was sealed that very minute. The Da Vinci taken out of a plain black bag by Bouvier had an indelible effect. Bouvier then transferred $20 million to Sotheby's as an intermediary, paying a total of $83 million for the painting, with an agreed sale price of $127,5 million. Bouvier made $44,5 million on the painting but saved Rybolovlev, who had planned to buy the Da Vinci for $190 million, $62,5 million.

Rybolovlev was saying that he planned to hang the painting in his home, in his oval room, but never did.

In 2014, Bouvier resold to Rybolovlev for €140m (equivalent $189 million) the 1951 masterpiece by Mark Rothko's *No. 6 (Violet, Green, and Red)*, which he purchased for a "mere" $80 million.

In anticipation of generating a new $109 million in revenue, in September 2014 he opened a Freeport in Luxembourg, not as big as the one in Singapore. As observed by *The Economist*, these were "*über* warehouses for the ultra-rich." Bouvier planned to set up analogous Freeports in Dubai and Shanghai. Money was needed for all these undertakings, and Bouvier had the money that he was receiving from Rybolovlev. There was little left to do: sell to Rybolovlev some more paintings.

It was difficult to find a painting for sale. Sometimes Rybolovlev demanded a particular painting, and it took years of searching to find out who owned it and convince the owners to give it away. "The work of an art dealer is like hunting," Bouvier was saying. "You need to know the right places, to be able to wait for the right moment, to approach quietly, so as not to frighten the seller, not to tremble when the opportunity presents itself". One of the gems of Rybolovlev's collection—Gauguin's *Otahi*—has not appeared on the market since before the war. It took years to find a trace of it. Klimt's "Water Snakes II" was a forced sale after Hitler annexed Austria. It was necessary to find the previous owners, to compensate the ten heirs and the foundation that owned the painting. The lady who kept the painting was very old, so a medical examination was required to make her consent legally valid. Permission had to be obtained so that the work could then leave the country. Rothko's painting *No. 6 (Purple, Green, and Red)* belonged to the Moueix family of the Bordeaux wine-making dynasty that owned the legendary Petrus estate. Jean-Pierre Moueix was a renowned collector and it was he who acquired the painting. After he died in 2003, it took years of negotiations to convince his heirs to sell it.

This painting was the last deal between Bouvier and Rybolovlev, and Bouvier never received the full amount he was promised: $60 million Rybolovlev held as leverage for future talks.

In the summer of 2014, in the presence of Rappo, Bouvier met with Rybolovlev on Scorpios to discuss this debt. Rybolovlev said he was having cash flow problems and asked Bouvier to sell some paintings from his collection, much to Bouvier's puzzlement. Bouvier had by then printed a catalog of Rybolovlev's collection, including the Rothko painting, not realizing that he would never have a chance to present this album to his client:

on 9 January 2015, Rybolovlev, without telling Bouvier, filed a complaint against him with the Monegasque court, accusing Bouvier of fraud. So, Rybolovlev was left without a gift. Bouvier kept the album.

"The relationship was broken after he asked me to engage in some illegal activities," Bouvier said to me during our conversation. "I refused to bribe the judges who heard Rybolovlev's divorce case."

Rybolovlev was ordered to pay $4,5 billion as part of the divorce. In August 2014, in the presence of Bersheda, who acted as interpreter, Rybolovlev told Bouvier the following: "Yves, I helped you gain your business footing. Now you need to help me save my fortune. I want to make sure that the appeal I am filing is decided in my favor. You can do whatever you want. You can use dirt, corruption—whatever you want. But you need to influence the judges."

In August 2014, Rybolovlev met with Bouvier at his villa on the French Riviera. The meeting was also attended by the oligarch's lawyer Bersheda. Rybolovlev asked Bouvier to help bribe the judges who would hear an appeal against a court ruling requiring him to pay Yelena $4,5 billion. He asked Bouvier to find vulnerabilities in magistrates involved in Rybolovlev's divorce proceedings, whether financial, sexual, or corruption-related issues, to prepare for possible blackmail. "There is no limit to what I can pay," Rybolovlev told Bouvier. "I have made a lot of money with you, but I am not ready to go to jail. Therefore, I can't do that. It is illegal to bribe judges in Switzerland," Bouvier replied and hoped Rybolovlev would not revisit the issue.

However, on 6 October 2014, Bersheda handed Bouvier a handwritten note with the names of the judges he was to influence and the number of the lawsuit. When Bouvier arrived in Monaco on 25 November for Rybolovlev's birthday, the latter spoke again about the judges and added: "If you don't help me, before Christmas you will return all the money for all the paintings you sold me." The conversation was translated by Bogdanov.

Given that the paintings could not be sold at that time because they were under arrest due to divorce, and it was impossible to sell this kind of artwork in a month in all cases, Rybolovlev's threat sounded absurd. "Either you do it or you'll be in trouble," he finished.

Bouvier approached the problem in a cool and businesslike manner. He analyzed each painting and wrote down how it should be sold to increase its value. He wrote to Sotheby's asking them to help him develop a strategy for selling the paintings in the Rybolovlev collection. Some, presumably, were better sold through public auctions. Some through auctions, but as private sales. For example, the painting "Martyrdom of St Sebastian" by El Greco, bought by Rybolovlev for €39,2 million, Bouvier proposed to sell not at auction, but privately, through private sales. Rybolovlev gave the painting to a public auction, and it was not sold.

On 12 January, Bersheda filed a lawsuit with the Prosecutor General's Office on behalf of Accent Delight International LTD and Xitrans Finances LTD, two offshore companies based in the British Virgin Islands and held in trust under Cypriot law, one of the beneficiaries of which was Rybolovlev's eldest daughter. In the filing, Rybolovlev claimed that, according to the agreement between them, Bouvier was Rybolovlev's agent, working for a 2% commission on the price of the paintings he bought.

It was later on proven that, in breach of all rules and ethical standards, the Monaco prosecutor had reviewed a draft of the filing and provided recommendations to Bersheda about its content.

On 12 January, the same day the complaint was filed, Christophe Haget, chief superintendent and head of the Criminal Investigation Department, and Frédéric Fusari, chief inspector of police, were ordered to report to the office of public prosecutor Jean-Pierre Dréno. There, Bersheda was waiting for them. Dréno handed the officers Bersheda's complaint and a warrant to investigate and ordered that the investigation be conducted as soon as possible.

Haget later wrote that he and his colleague, following their superiors' instructions, completed the investigation quickly, although they felt they needed more time and should have been more cautious in their conclusions.

Events unfolded dramatically. On 14 January, direct telephone contact was established between Bersheda and Haget. Until February 2015, Bersheda supervised the work of the police officers investigating Bouvier's complaint daily, constantly meeting with them herself or together with Rybolovlev, either at the police station or at Rybolovlev's villa. These contacts then continued until January 2016.

For the weekend of 20-22 February, Rybolovlev invited Justice Minister Philippe Narmino and his wife Christine to stay at his chalet in Gstaad. They flew there and back in a specially chartered luxury helicopter. "Thanks again, dear Tetiana, for the wonderful WE [weekend] in your company," Christina Narmina wrote to Bersheda on 22 February. "Please thank Dmitri on our behalf for his unfailing hospitality and pass on our warmest feelings of friendship and our congratulations on the beauty of his home in Gstaad. Good night and see you soon.—Ph & Ch."

Bersheda responded: "Thank you very much too! It was a great pleasure spending the weekend with you and skiing together! I won't fail to pass on your message to Dmitri who was delighted to receive you in his home. Have a good evening. Hugs. Tetiana."

Gerard Cohen, managing director of HSBC's private bank in Monaco, was also present at Rybolovlev's chalet that weekend. The fact is that Tania Rappo and her husband Jacques-Olivier Rappo, Elena Rybolovleva's dentist, whom the Rybolovlevs had befriended in Geneva, where the Rappos were living at the time, had accounts at this bank.

Rappo was a publisher with connections in the Swiss elite. Being of Bulgarian descent, she spoke fluent Russian and helped the Rybolovlevs, and especially Dmitri, who did not speak any foreign languages, in their daily lives. The relationship was so friendly that Tania Rappo became godmother to the Rybolovlevs' youngest daughter Anna, born in Geneva in 2001. The girl's godfather was Vladimir Shevtsov, who traveled from Russia for the purpose.

"My first impression was that he was a very reserved man, very cold," Rappo said of Rybolovlev. "But I found him interesting. I grew up in Russian literature. I'm a Russophile, I like a lot of things about Russia. Let's just say something was intriguing about him, and his story was intriguing too. I thought he was smart. I was much closer to his wife; we were friends with his wife. With him, we developed a certain relationship. By the time he started talking about the paintings, he had already asked me for a few different contacts that put him in touch with people in the wine business, diamond business, and biotechnology. You know, every time he had an idea, he would ask me if I knew people in those areas, and if I could, I would introduce him."

So, this was Tania Rappo who introduced Rybolovlev to Bouvier.

"I introduced him to people," she continued her story, "and one day he said he intended to put together a collection, to buy paintings. I remember very well how he visited a business partner in Canada, in whose house he was very impressed by the paintings on the walls, and said to me that he would be interested in buying the paintings. And he asked me if I knew any people from whom he could buy paintings. I wasn't in the art world. I was editing books. I didn't know what the art trade was at all, but since he insisted on it, I remembered that I had friends who had a gallery. I introduced him to them and he bought a painting. When he bought the first painting in that gallery, which had nothing to do with Bouvier, he asked me to go with him to the Geneva Freeport to pick up the [Marc Chagall] painting. At that time, I didn't even know what a Freeport was. It was the first time I discovered the Freeport and learned that there was such an institution. And so, at Freeport, we met a gentleman (I didn't remember his name) who was supposed to organize all the paperwork. Rybolovlev received his painting, and two or three days later Mr. Bouvier called me. He somehow found my phone and suggested we have a coffee. We had coffee and he said:

"Well, I understand that Mr. Rybolovlev wants to buy paintings. Can you arrange for me to do business with him?"

To which I replied: "OK. But why don't you call him directly?"

Bouvier said: "Well, first of all, I don't have his phone number. And then, I'm very afraid that I wouldn't dare to ask him for such a rendezvous. You know, please arrange it for me, and if, one day, a painting is sold, there will be something for you too. There will be a commission, as usual in this business."

I didn't believe this. But I called Rybolovlev and told him: "There is a man who wants to meet you since you told me that you want to buy paintings. He wants to sell you paintings. Do you want to meet him?"

Rybolovlev replied: "Immediately!"

And we went to see Bouvier that same day.

When I organized the meeting, I thought I was doing Rybolovlev a much bigger favor than to Bouvier."

After that meeting with Bouvier, Rybolovlev whispered in Tania's ear: "He is exactly the man I need."

But circumstances have changed. In early 2015, Rybolovlev had new plans for Bouvier and Rappo. It was now necessary to show that Bouvier and Rappo were accomplices conducting their business in Monaco, where Rybolovlev now lived.

In an official document dated 17 February 2015, provided to Monaco prosecutors when they were preparing to arrest Bouvier, the names of Tania Rappo's husband Jacques-Olivier Rappo, and Yves Bouvier in bank statements were deliberately changed to make it appear that Bouvier and Tania Rappo had four accounts in common and to suggest money laundering and concealment in Monaco to which Tania Rappo, who lived in Monaco, might have been theoretically involved, but to which Bouvier, a Swiss citizen, had nothing to do even in theory.

For this purpose, three directors of Mopaso's HSBC bank signed fabricated documents and sent them to the police under their signatures. When it later transpired that the documents had been forged, HSBC attributed this to a "clerical error." It was based on this "error" that Bouvier was brought under Monaco jurisdiction and could now be arrested in Monaco.

On 23 February 2015, Rybolovlev invited Tania Rappo to dinner at his home in La Belle Époque. Bersheda was also invited. The table was sumptuous—with caviar, wine and vodka. Rappo even had the impression that she was being deliberately drunk. It turned out that Bersheda had been recording the dinner conversation on her phone to be used as forensic evidence, and had been spiking Tania's drink to get her to talk more. At the end of the dinner, Rybolovlev asked Rappo to invite Bouvier to his house on 25 February so that they could discuss the pending issues. Bouvier agreed, anticipating that he would finally receive the underpaid $60 million for Rothko.

As with the arrest of Elena Rybolovleva, who was arrested in Cyprus a year ago, Bersheda coordinated the "operation." She informed the Monegasque police of the exact time of Bouvier's arrival at Rybolovleva's house. Bouvier flew from Geneva to Nice in the early hours of 25 February in a private jet, got to Monaco in a black Mercedes with a driver, and wandered around the port a bit to admire the boats as he arrived early, but at exactly 10 am, as agreed, rang the bell at the door of the building.

"When I pressed the doorbell," Bouvier recalled, "two men rushed at me. For a second, I thought they were Dmitry's bodyguards. But they showed me their police IDs and.. handcuffed me, squeezed me very tightly... I found out later that they were agents from the drug squad. Then they took me in a car to the police headquarters. When we arrived, one of the men said to me, "Put a scarf over your hands, so one can't see the handcuffs." I didn't understand anything that was happening to me."

The police officers who arrested Bouvier were nine in number. They were indeed from the narcotics division. Bouvier was charged with fraud and money laundering.

Rappo was arrested the same day.

"The police came," she later recalled, "showed me some papers. There were a lot of police officers there. And I looked at the papers and I saw the name of Mr. Rybolovlev's trust. And I can tell you that I—I'm a lady of age. I've never had a problem with the justice system, I've never even had a driving ticket. I've managed to live to a ripe old age with no problems. And I had I don't know how many cops at my door. I was in shock. If I hadn't known about the story with his wife's ring in Cyprus I probably would have died. I think that's what saved my life. When I saw his name on the envelope, and I saw those policemen, I thought this was just another one of those strange inventions that he just made. I didn't know what it was. But somehow it saved me because, from that moment in Cyprus, I got the feeling that this was a man with great manipulative abilities and quite a cynical person.

In the complaint which they filed against Bouvier, my name wasn't even mentioned. I was victimized because I lived in Monaco. Mr. Rybolovlev had some kind of complaints against Mr. Bouvier about the paintings. But no paintings have crossed the borders of Monaco. Mr. Rybolovlev's companies were offshore. They had nothing to do with Monaco. Mr. Bouvier's company, the seller's company, was an offshore company. All of them had nothing to do with Monaco. This story had no reason to take place in Monaco. But Mr. Rybolovlev was desperate to link this case to Monaco. My only fault is that I live in Monaco and that I get commissions from their deals, legitimate commissions. But I am a resident of Monaco. So, the only reason the whole story was Monaco-related was because of my involvement in it. Even though I wasn't in the complaint.

And after that, even more incredible things happen. I find myself in this story with forged documents from HSBC Bank. The bank, where Mr. Rybolovlev was a very big client, produced false, forged papers saying that I have common companies with Mr. Bouvier, which is untrue. And they replaced my husband's name in the documents with Mr. Bouvier's name, which is completely unbelievable. So, they said that if I had companies with

Mr. Bouvier, the fact that I received money from the commission and then invested it in companies with Bouvier could be a reason for an investigation, which is complete nonsense."

On 26 February, Haget sent a message to Bersheda with an update on the case:

"Tetiana, we will use tomorrow's appearances in court to insist on Monaco's jurisdiction. We have been working to ensure the extension of the GAV [custodial orders] by the JLD [bail court judge] at tomorrow's hearing…We are meeting around 10 am to discuss all aspects of the case. Have a good evening. Christophe."

Rybolovlev's lawyers asserted that Bouvier cheated their client out of a non-round sum of $1.049.465.009.

Let's clarify some of the numbers. When Rybolovlev's lawyers determined the amount of the loss, they had no way of knowing Bouvier's purchase prices, except for the single Modigliani painting bought by Bouvier from Steven Cohen, which, at least formally, is what started the scandal. If we can agree that Rybolovlev invested $2 billion in the paintings bought from Bouvier (although in reality, this figure was less, $1,8 billion), then the claim that Bouvier earned a billion from Rybolovlev is incorrect. Bouvier's income from reselling artworks to Rybolovlev was approximately $325 million. This is not small money, but it is still not a billion. 5% of the sale price of all the paintings—$90 million, based on a total of $1,8 billion (not $2 billion)—Bouvier paid the middleman who introduced him to Rybolovlev, Tania Rappo. This was the custom in the art world: if someone brought a buyer to a gallery, he got 10% for it. In Rappo's case, a verbal agreement was reached for 5% of all the sums Bouvier received from Rybolovlev.

"Bouvier was very honest with me," Rappo recalled. "When I introduced him to Rybolovlev, Bouvier said that every time he would buy a painting from him, I would receive a commission. I didn't believe him, especially since I had no contract with him. So, Bouvier paid a commission every time he sold a painting. But when I introduced Rybolovlev to him, no one expected that this guy [Rybolovlev] would buy $2 billion worth of paintings. My commission was 5%. It was a lot of money, crazy money. But it was a normal commission in the art world—between 5% and 10%. Sometimes he'd give me more, sometimes less. He could stop at any minute. But anyone who knows Bouvier, who has worked with him, knows that he is a man who does business on a handshake. He never cheated anyone, never. He had the profile of a man of the old school. He had a fantastic reputation in the business. I had no contract with him. He already knew Rybolovlev, he could have said to me: "You've got enough money already". He behaved the same way with other people, not only with me."

It is fair to point out that Rybolovlev, judging by the lawsuits, never complained about the prices at which he bought the paintings. He agreed that Bouvier's prices were fair. The claim was that Bouvier was not supposed to make money on it, but was obliged, according to Rybolovlev, to receive a 2% commission on sales, which from the total turnover of $1,8 billion would amount to $36 million. Given that Bouvier paid $90 million in commission to Rappo alone, such a statement of the matter was absurd. Rybolovlev, if we agree with his logic and figures, overpaid Bouvier $289 million, but still—not a billion.

Bouvier's arrest in Monaco had nothing to do with the paintings and the "two billion" paid to Bouvier but had everything to do with Bouvier's Freeports, which Rybolovlev planned to reissue to his structures. Therefore, Rybolovlev's lawyers deliberately inflated the amount for damages, using estimates that were in no way based on expert analyses and real numbers. Rybolovlev wanted a fabulously high claim amount so that it could include absolutely everything Bouvier owned, including the Singapore and Luxembourg Freeports. If a Singapore court were to recognize the validity of Rybolovlev's administrative claim against Bouvier for, say, $1 billion, it would mean that all of Bouvier's assets would pass to Rybolovlev, including the Luxembourg and Singapore ports.

As Bouvier was saying, "Rybolovlev's attacks against me had nothing to do with the sale of art (...) Firstly, he was half-way through the most expensive divorce in history and wanted to depreciate the value of his art collection. Secondly, he wanted to punish me for having refused to corrupt Swiss judges for his very expensive divorce. Thirdly, he wanted to steal my freeport business in Singapore and build his own for the Russian Federation in Vladivostok."[57]

No art collector in the world would ever claim to have overpaid a piece of art—this is unheard of. Every art collector claims that he underpaid, with the view or reselling his art at a higher price later on. Rybolovlev highly unusual move, presenting himself as an ignorant art collector, shows that the dispute with Bouvier had nothing to do with Bouvier's role as an art dealer.

On 12 March 2015, Rybolovlev's company filed an application for a worldwide order freezing Bouvier's assets and those of his companies and compensating Rybolovlev for the $1.1 billion in damages caused by Bouvier in Singapore, where Bouvier's Freeport was located, and in Hong Kong.

So, Bouvier was lured to Monaco, arrested, and put in a cell. Rybolovlev believed that a Monaco judge he bribed would order Bouvier to be held in custody pending a court verdict (which could take three months). And while Bouvier would be in a Monaco prison, Rybolovlev, who had more opportunities in Monaco, would force him to sign a plea bargain and hand over the Freeports to pay for the losses. Such a system of property seizure was routinely practiced in Russia. In this sense, Rybolovlev did not invent anything new, but merely used his own and other people's Russian experience, and most importantly, repeated the same operation that he had just carried out not too successfully with his wife, who was arrested in the presence of Bouvier in Cyprus.

Bouvier and Rappo were questioned on charges of fraud and money laundering. The authorities charged them and intended to keep them in custody for some time. But Bouvier was lucky: three days later, after interrogations and a confrontation with Rybolovlev, during which, according to Bouvier, Rybolovlev avoided looking him in the eye, Bouvier was released on €10 million bail by a judge who was not "his own man" and did not know about Rybolovlev's collusion with the Monegasque police. Rappo was released at the same time.

Bouvier immediately left Monaco and filed counterclaims against Rybolovlev. Eyewitnesses said that Rybolovlev was furious at the incompetence and stupidity of his underlings who had let Bouvier getaway. Having realized that the plan to take the Freeports from Bouvier had failed, Rybolovlev immediately flew to Moscow to coordinate further actions with his partners.

It must be said that Rybolovlev had been preparing for this operation for a long time, and Bouvier's arrest was not something spontaneous. A scheme for Bouvier's arrest was agreed with the Monegasque police in advance. A communiqué on his arrest was prepared in advance, and by someone's inadvertence, this communiqué was released to the press even before the arrest took place. Rybolovlev also hired a retired former head of the French secret service to guarantee access to classified information related to his court cases. He hired a PR man who worked for the French Ministry of Defense, believing that this would enable him to control the French media. He employed six detectives to follow Bouvier (they did follow him). Through lawyers, after Bouvier's release from Monegasque prison, he has frozen all of Bouvier's finances. He sent letters to all important people in the world of art, threatening them with complications if they continued to cooperate with Bouvier, as they would then be considered to be accomplices in the crimes. He wrote denunciations against Bouvier to the tax police and published articles denigrating Bouvier in the press.

Rybolovlev and Bersheda ran a massive black PR campaign against Bouvier all around the world. In addition, all lawyers working for Bouvier were the target of hacking attacks.

Rybolovlev did not realize that in Switzerland the system of justice and power did not work the same way as in Perm or even Monaco or Cyprus. "One evening in Switzerland, I accompanied Dmitry and Elena to a dinner with businessmen and lawyers, members of Geneva's upper middle class," Tania Rappo recounted. "Explaining why he was disappointed with Switzerland, Rybolovlev said: "When I was in Russia, I thought your country was the only real capitalist country in Europe. I thought people with money had power, and controlled the justice system, the police, and the government. But you have referendums and you have socialists in parliament.""

Rybolovlev was sincerely convinced that everyone and everywhere could be bought, that if he allowed Bouvier to earn money Bouvier would become his slave, especially since Rybolovlev was holding a hostage: a $60 million payment for that Rothko. "To explain to Rybolovlev that in Switzerland, the moment you walk up to a judge to say, "Look, you can earn something..." you are immediately arrested and imprisoned, was impossible," Bouvier said.

After his short-term arrest and then release in Monaco in 2015, Bouvier, of course, cut off all contact with Rybolovlev. But while in custody, when the confrontation between Rybolovlev and Bouvier ended and both signed all relevant protocols, Bouvier told Rybolovlev that he was ready to buy back all the masterpieces sold to him at the original price if he would have one year to find the money for the purchase. Rybolovlev flatly refused the offer.

Bouvier did indeed open Freeports on the profits from reselling the paintings to Rybolovlev. However, he did not care how much he overpaid for the paintings since these were not expenses but investments: the more he invested in Bouvier, the larger would be the return. He once happened to divulge to the Swiss investigators precisely this: that he "invested" a billion dollars in Bouvier. Now came the time to collect the return on his investment.

It is possible to imagine that being as savvy as he is, having experienced a Russian prison, having built his successful business in Russia during "the wild 1990s," having become a billionaire, and having left Russia with his capital intact, Rybolovlev was not aware of what he was doing and was simply giving away hundreds of millions of dollars to Bouvier.

On 21 August 2015, a Singapore court dismissed Rybolovlev's lawsuit against Bouvier to freeze his assets. On 4 September 2015, a Hong Kong court also dismissed Rybolovlev's lawsuit. Since then, the lawsuits filed by Rybolovlev and his companies against Bouvier gradually began to lose momentum, and Bouvier and Rappo went on the offensive.

In August 2015, a criminal investigation was opened in Geneva against Rybolovlev and Bersheda on charges of corruption based on a criminal complaint filed by Bouvier. The complaint explained that Rybolovlev and Bersheda had asked Bouvier to influence appeals judges ruling on the multi-billion-dollar divorce proceedings between Elena and Dmitry Rybolovlev. Bouvier found in his possession, which took some time, and gave to the Geneva prosecutor's office the very handwritten note with the list of judges and case number that Bersheda had given him. Her fingerprints were preserved and identified on the note. Bersheda admitted that she had given Bouvier the list, but claimed that this was to verify that the judges had no conflict of interest.

A Swiss prosecutor investigated the case for two years and found that the events as described by Bouvier were accurate: "The handing over of the list.. confirms Bouvier's allegation that he was asked to bribe and/or black-mail the judges hearing Rybolovlev's appeal against the first-instance court judgment in the divorce case, by any means and regardless of the costs," the prosecutor wrote in his legal opinion.

Meanwhile, Tania Rappo filed a criminal complaint against Bersheda for illegally recording a private conversation with her about Bouvier at

Rybolovlev's La Belle Epoque home on 23 February 2015, because while in police custody, Rappo learned that Bersheda had given police a CD containing excerpts of the conversation. On 26 February, while Bouvier and Rappo were still in custody, a printout of the French translation of the conversation was forwarded by Bersheda from her phone to the French investigators investigating Bouvier and Rappo. Rappo therefore filed a complaint against Rybolovlev, Bersheda, and HSBC for conspiracy to arrest her and breach of privacy because Rybolovlev and Bersheda recorded her conversation without her consent.

In the small state of Monaco, under the Franco-Monaco agreement, judges are sent from France. Rappo's complaint was investigated by magistrate Edouard Levraurt, who had just been seconded to Monaco and was not involved in Rybolovlev's collusion. After examining the evidence presented to him, the magistrate decided that Rappo's complaint of entrapment was valid and launched an investigation. In late 2015, Levraurt asked Bersheda to hand over the phone from which the conversation with Rappo had been recorded, to see if the original recording matched the information on the compact disc that Bersheda had given to the police.

Levraurt passed the messages found on Bersheda's phone to his colleague Judge Morgan Raymond, who was investigating Rybolovlev's complaint. Based on these messages, a report was compiled stating that Bouvier's arrest was a conspiracy orchestrated by Rybolovlev with the assistance of his lawyer, the principality's justice minister, the police chief, and officers.

The report stated that Bersheda informed police officers Haget and Fusari of Bouvier's movements and his planned visit (at her invitation) to Monaco. On 23 February 2015, she alerted the officers that Bouvier would arrive in Monaco two days later:

"Good evening. He will be coming on the 25th in the morning. That's for sure. We should stick to plan A. Please call me back when you can. Thanks, Tetiana."

The next day she also messaged Fusari: "Bouvier has confirmed the meeting for tomorrow at 10.00. Could you please call me back?"

On 2 March, well after Bouvier's release from prison, Bersheda wrote again to the officers:

"Hello. I hope you had a good weekend. Will you be in the office today? DR [Dmitry Rybolovlev] would like to pass by to see if you have an update and discuss what's next before his departure tomorrow from MC [Monaco] for one week. Thanks in advance. Tetiana."

In February 2016, Bersheda was charged and detained. She was investigated on charges of violation of privacy. The phone handed over by Bersheda to the prosecutors had all messages deleted beforehand. The magistrate ordered a thorough forensic examination of the phone, and in July 2016 investigators were able to recover all the deleted texts, including some 8900 SMS messages from 20 July 2013 to 17 November 2015. The content of these messages revealed Rybolovlev's tactics and intrigues, confirming that Monaco and Cyprus are the two states where Rybolovlev got away with everything.

Released on bail, Bersheda fled from Monaco to London, having emptied her Monegasque bank account of €17 million.

However, it was Rybolovlev, not his ex-wife, who won as far as finances were concerned. In June 2015, an appeals court ruled that Elena had no jurisdiction over family trusts registered in Cyprus and ordered Rybolovlev to pay his ex-wife a much smaller sum: CHF 564 million (€534 million). This happened against the backdrop of an open investigation initiated by Bouvier's lawsuit. For some time, the prosecutor's office tried to determine whether the new agreement on such a low amount was not the result of pressure exerted on the Swiss court by Rybolovlev. It ruled that it was not. In October 2015, Elena agreed to an undisclosed settlement with Dmitry and a mutual dismissal of the litigation. Presumably, including the divorce money, Rybolovleva could have received about $1 billion. The most expensive and scandalous divorce proceedings in the history of mankind were finalized, although Rybolovlev still did not pay some part of the total amount, leaving it as leverage to put pressure on Elena in the future.

When Judge Raymond called Rybolovlev to testify under oath in July 2017, he asked him if he had claimed that there were three places in the world where he could do whatever he wanted: Cyprus, Skorpios, and Monaco. He also asked him how the police knew he would meet with Bouvier in his house in Monaco, why they were waiting for Bouvier on his doorstep, and why he accused Bouvier of defrauding him of artworks belonging to the Domus Trust based in Cyprus, while he had claimed in writing in his other court case that the masterpieces never belonged to him but to the trust.

Following the legal difficulties, Rybolovlev began to contemplate a plan to sell his paintings and in 2017 he began rapidly selling off the collection he had amassed at apparently undervalued prices. This may also have been due to a desire to quickly depreciate the value of his collection for the duration of his divorce.

At the sale of the first three masterpieces through Christie's auction in February 2017, Rybolovlev lost an estimated $100 million.[58] On the sale of the next four, another $150 million.[59]

By that time, the art world, probably not without Rybolovlev's "black PR" concerning Bouvier, was abuzz with rumors that Bouvier sold all of the paintings to Rybolovlev at prices that were inflated two-fold, and now Rybolovlev, being in dire straits, had to sell his masterpieces at a significant loss. Still, it was then that the experts began suspecting that Rybolovlev's art purchases were made with ulterior motives that had little to do with collecting or investing. How else can one explain the $10,4 million purchase by Rybolovlev of a bronze Rodin sculpture that was produced in 2010?[60]

"There are two types of art objects," Bouvier philosophized. "The first type was bought to decorate something. And the second type he bought as an investment. Anything by Rodin, Mayol, another Rodin, it was to decorate a terrace in Monaco or a flat in Monaco, because he wanted to put them by the pool. He wanted to decorate his place. The Rodin he bought for 8 million—a normal person would spend 100 francs on it, roughly speaking. For Rybolovlev, these art objects were just decorations for his home. He bought a flat in Monaco for 320 million. Spending 20-30 million on jewelry, including Rodin, is not a problem for him."

According to Bouvier, on the resale of paintings, if Rybolovlev listened to advice, he could earn up to a billion dollars. For example, he bought from Bouvier three nude paintings by Modigliani for $160 million. Two other nude paintings by Modigliani, which did not belong to Rybolovlev, were later sold at auction for $340 million. Van Gogh, bought from Bouvier for $17 million and resold it for $53 million. Picasso's *Musketeer with a Pipe* was bought for $12,5 million, and he resold it for $30 million. Klimt purchased for $183 million, he sold through a private sale only slightly higher, for about $200 million, but for about another $200 million he sold, also privately, bought from Bouvier for $43,8 million Picasso's painting *The Wedding of Pierrette (Les Noces de Pierrette)*. He ended up selling about $1,2 billion worth of art, making somewhere around $320 million, and he still had plenty left over (for example, he initially bought six Picasso paintings through Bouvier).

With the loss, the Magritte painting had to be sold. In 2013, it was promised to be loaned to the MoMA (Museum of Modern Art) in New York for an exhibition. They even managed to print a catalog with Magritte included in it. But at the last moment, Rybolovlev refused to give the painting to the museum because of the upcoming dismantling, fearing that the painting would be seized. Then Bouvier, to save the reputation of the museum, which remains without Magritte, issued a so-called "state guarantee," i.e. a document issued by the US government and insuring the owner against any sanctions against his property. But despite this, Rybolovlev refused to give the painting to the exhibition. In 2015, there was a big Magritte exhibition at the Pompidou Museum in Paris. But Rybolovlev refused to give the painting there as well. And when he eventually put it up for sale, potential buyers refused to buy it at market price because they thought there was a problem with the painting not having been in two Magritte exhibitions, in New York and Paris. There was no problem with the painting. The problem was with Rybolovlev.

Another Picasso piece Rybolovlev was trying to sell in London, while Bouvier, together with Christie's, wrote to Rybolovlev that a painting of that size should be sold in New York. Had Rybolovlev agreed to wait just four months, he would have successfully sold his Picasso in New York, but he stuck to his judgment, auctioned it in London, and failed.

"Each of his paintings has a price that another is willing to pay to buy it back," Bouvier said.—Dimitri has really extraordinary paintings. If his collection loses value, it will be his fault alone: he himself provoked this scandal. If you shout everywhere that your paintings are not worth what you paid for them, they have already lost their value."

However, the rapid sale of paintings could have been caused by very different reasons. Rybolovlev's divorce was creating unnecessary noise and drawing unwanted attention to both Rybolovlev and his money. Rybolovlev was lucky because the potash business is not the kind of business that attracted attention from outsiders and that everyone dreamed of. It is fertilizer, not gold, diamonds or oil. Although he became very rich, he managed to escape the spotlight because other businesses involved in oil, gas and metals attracted more attention than fertilizers.

But assuming that Rybolovlev could also be a custodian of other people's money or was buying masterpieces for his partners, amid numerous counter-suits, such as Bouvier's billion-dollar lawsuit against Rybolovlev, the partners might have been afraid for their investments and demanded their immediate return. Rybolovlev's partners were very serious and very high-ranking, and it was deadly dangerous to come into conflict with them.

Always suspecting everyone, he led a clandestine lifestyle, venturing out of his tight inner circle only to meet with his attorney and a hairdresser. Outside of his house, he always appeared in the company of eight body-guards fearing for his life. His chalet in Gstaad, Switzerland, had a panic room with armored walls and bulletproof blacked-out windows, and it was impossible to see what was going on inside from the outside. When talking to someone in his own home, he chose the most protected place, preferably not by the window. On his first superyacht "Anna I", registered in the Cayman Islands, 67 meters (220 feet) long and worth $65 million (Rybolovlev owned her from 2007 to 2021), he made his cabin upstairs, without windows, so that he could not be seen from outside. In the restau-rant, all bottles and even yogurts had to be opened in front of him, other-wise he would not touch them because he feared being poisoned. His wife Elena thought that he was afraid of the mafia because after the sale of Uralkali, he did not pay them back. It was hard for her to suppose that Rybolovlev was one of the leaders of the very Mafia he had always feared.

"When you leave Russia with so much money, and with all the spending that Rybolovlev had, it's impossible to cut all your ties with Russia," Bouvier said about Rybolovlev. "He was meeting with Putin. He was flying to Trutnev's birthdays."

But there was another person that Rybolovlev never told us about. This person was General Ezubchenko.

It turned out that as of 2002 the General's fortune was estimated at €7,5 billion, and when selling Uralkali he earned €2,5 billion (this was his share—about 33%). It followed from all this that the total price for Uralkali was higher than $9 billion. That was exactly what Bouvier believed:

"Rybolovlev sold Uralkali. But that was not all he had. He had other potash-related companies, and his business interests in potash continued. He also had companies related to trading. Most of the profits from Uralkali were withdrawn to other companies. Uralkali's main customer was China because they needed fertilizer. Everything related to dealing with China was handled by an intermediary company, and the profits were deposited in China. Officially Rybolovlev sold Uralkali for $7-8-9 billion, but everything related to these intermediary organizations, where the profits were deposited, he sold later. Those who bought Uralkali didn't need just Uralkali, they needed everything. So, there was a lot more money there. Maybe it wasn't his money, but in any case, there was a lot more money there.

Collectors don't usually invest more than 10% of their wealth in art. People keep money often to invest in the stock market, to invest in a new business, or in some financial products. But to spend that much and to spend it so easily is very strange, and that's why I'm sure that the two billion was not a quarter of Rybolovlev's total money. I'm sure he has some sort of piggy bank that he has access to, where there's a lot more money than what is officially known. Much, much, much more money in there. He bought a new yacht for $250 million. He's going to build another yacht that he told me about in 2014, "That's expensive, 800 million it costs. It's expensive." If you have only 6-7 billion, spending 800 million on a toy is an impossible thing. The important question is how much of his fortune he invested in art. This is very unusual behavior given that he spent a lot of money on paintings."

It was about the construction in Holland of the 110-metre (360-foot) superyacht Anna II, then registered, like Rybolovlev's first yacht, in the Cayman Islands. She was purchased by Rybolovlev in 2018. It is believed to have cost "only" $250-300 million (actually around $500 million), but still not $800 million. Rybolovlev sold the Anna-I yacht in 2021 and bought a $20 million racing yacht, Skorpios, instead.

"As for his official assets, his official fortune, which has been estimated at 6-7 billion," Bouvier continued, "either he has a lot more unaccounted money or he lives on credit. Because otherwise, it's impossible to make ends meet with all the spending he does. If you have a fortune of 6 billion, you can't spend two billion on art and paintings and another two billion on property. Everything about his toys—football, yachts, airplanes—that's another billion. And one billion to pay his wife for the divorce. Mathematically, it doesn't add up. Of the 6 billion he got, two billion according to his wife was sent to some company. It's not clear what kind of company it was—Trutnev's, Lukashenko's, or someone else's, but those two billion—they went somewhere. It is impossible to spend that much if you have, roughly speaking, four billion. Either he has much more money, or what he spends doesn't belong to him.

What's strange is that when he resumed buying in 2010, he was buying paintings that cost twice as much as the previous ones, while spending half as much time evaluating the painting. It is difficult to find a logical explanation for this. I don't know the answer to that question. It seems to me that it was someone else [through Rybolovlev] who invested money in the paintings."

There was another baffling moment as well. In 2008, Rybolovlev asked Bouvier to make copies of three paintings he had previously bought. The copies in question were made so professionally that only an expert, having turned the painting over and studied the canvas, could realize that he was dealing with a copy and not with the original. The average person could not distinguish a copy from the original, of course. Each copy cost from 50 to 100 thousand to make it took 3-4 months, and there was only one person who knew how to do it—Brazilian artist-copyist Flavio, who had long worked with Bouvier and knew him well. His services were usually used by clients who were selling their masterpieces but did not want anyone to know about them and therefore kept copies instead of the original.

Initially, it was thought that Rybolovlev would make copies of all the paintings he bought. However, after difficulties with the Sechin investigation and divorce in 2009, Rybolovlev stopped copying the paintings. Only three canvases were copied altogether, including one Modigliani out of seven. These were not the most expensive paintings in Rybolovlev's collection. There was no correlation between the price of the painting and the decision to copy it.

Bouvier casually mentioned Belarusian President Alexander Lukashenko because Rybolovlev became Lukashenko's most important strategic partner, as potash fertilizers were Belarus' second largest export product.

Belarusian potash fertilizers were sold through the Belarusian company Belaruskali. In 1992, A.G. Lomakin created the International Potash Company (IPC), which united the largest Russian potash fertilizer producers—Uralkali and Silvinit—and the Belarusian company Belaruskali, 100% owned by the state of Belarus, i.e. Lukashenko. In 1994, A. G. Lomakin became the general director of the ICC.

However, in 2005 the union broke up. "Uralkali" (represented by Rybolovlev) and "Belaruskali" (represented by Lukashenko) refused the services of the IPC, believing that A.G. Lomakin discriminated in favor of Silvinit, left the IPC and created their own joint company: "Belarusian Potash Company" (BPC), where 50% belonged to Uralkali, 45% to Belaruskali and 5% to Belarusian Railways, which took over the transportation of products.

The potash trade supported the Belarusian regime, and BKK helped provide Belarus with the hard currency cash flows it needed, especially after the US imposed wide-ranging sanctions against Lukashenko's regime. Rybolovlev thus became extremely important to the Kremlin as the manager of the main commercial relationship between Belarus and Russia.

"Belaruskali" became one of the world's largest producers of potash fertilizers. It was an international cartel that controlled about 42% of the global potash fertilizer market and ensured high market prices for the product. BPC exported up to 80% of its products to more than 50 countries.

In 2008, to improve BPC's position, Lukashenko granted the company significant tax incentives.

Lukashenko and Rybolovlev agreed on sales volumes, regulated potash production, and thus controlled potash and potash fertilizer prices. Several times a year Rybolovlev was not lazy to fly to Minsk for meetings with Lukashenko and visited him at his home. Secret meetings also took place in Germany in one of the clinics, where both came for examination and recovery. In Cyprus, Lukashenko and Rybolovlev spent time together on a yacht. According to Rybolovlev's wife, Lukashenko even offered her husband the post of trade minister. The financial component of the partnership was that Lukashenko gave Rybolovlev exclusive rights to trade in Belarusian potash, and billions of dollars, which was Lukashenko's share of the total profit, settled in Cyprus.

The billions of Ezubchenko, who, like Rybolovlev, was the main shareholder of the Bank of Cyprus, were also deposited there.

Maybe the paintings were bought for General Ezubchenko and that is why Rybolovlev asked him to move the paintings to Cyprus just before Bouvier's arrest in Monaco. Or maybe they were bought for Sergei Pavlovich Ezubchenko, the general's grandson?

The fact is that General Ezubchenko had two children: Pavel and Julia.

Over time, they also became officers of the FSB, and Pavel rose to the rank of major-general and the position of deputy head of the Department of Military Counterintelligence of the FSB. From 2006 to 2022, he was also Deputy Head of the Security Service of Sberbank of Russia.

Pavel Sergeevich Ezubchenko had a son named Sergei in honor of his grandfather. At the end of 2018, it was he who was given a stake in the Cypriot bank by his grandfather-general. By this time, however, the bank was badly battered. It had sheltered the wealth of many Russians and was linked to several scandals, including a €35 million loan to 13 members of the Cypriot parliament, who had not repaid either the debt or the interest. In March 2013, the bank suffered economic difficulties and faced a significant restructuring. Depositors with more than €100.000 in their accounts were part of the bank's recapitalization and lost around 30% of their funds. In 2014, the European Central Bank and the World Monetary Fund gave Cyprus €10 billion to rescue the banking sector. Under the deal, many wealthy Russian deposit holders lost their funds and became shareholders in the bank. Most of Rybolovlev's money in the bank melted away over time and he was left owning less than 1% of the bank's shares, which was not insignificant either.

But Sergei Ezubchenko (grandson) became one of the closest aides to Sergei Kiriyenko, first deputy head of the presidential administration and supervisor of the Kremlin's domestic policy. Ezubchenko's grandson also oversaw the entertainment division of the Gazprom-Media holding company. In addition to owning shares in the Bank of Cyprus since 2019, he was a business partner of Rybolovlev's daughters Ekaterina and Anna (who were his third cousins) in the Cypriot offshore Odella Resources Limited and several offshore companies registered in Montenegro and Luxembourg.

The brief official biography of Ezubchenko's grandson, which has no information before 2020, tells the following:

2020 г.—Assistant to the First Deputy Head of the Administration of the President of the Russian Federation Sergei Kiriyenko.

2020-2021.—First Deputy Director General of the Gazprom-Media Entertainment Television sub-holding.

2021-2022.—Advisor to Chairman of the Supervisory Board of Bosco di Ciliegi Group.

2022—Deputy General Director of Lukoil International Trading and Supply Company.

At the end of August 2022, Anton Vaino, Head of the Presidential Administration, signed an order appointing Ezubchenko's grandson to the position of Deputy Head of the Presidential Department for Domestic Policy.

Sergei Ezubchenko Jr. had been in public service for only about a year. According to his tax return, he did not acquire anything during this period—legally, he had neither a personal car nor a property. However, if you check the Russian Register, the picture is quite different. By that time he had managed to save up money for a 475-metre flat in the Moskva high-rise of the Moscow City complex (worth RUB 325.2 million) and a 493-metre flat in the Imperial House housing complex in Yakimanka district (worth RUB 612 million), a 305-metre flat in Ermolaevsky Lane near Patriarshy Ponds (worth RUB 227 million), a Mercedes-Benz S600 W222 Maybach, a BMW M760Li AT xDrive and a Mercedes-Benz S500 4MATIC, and a 327-metre villa in the Principality of Monaco, registered to the unemployed Natalia Mikhalkova, with whom Ezubchenko's grandson was romantically involved. The 2022 exchange rate was RUB 68 for $1.

Describing the fate of Ezubchenko's grandson we deliberately left one piquant detail for last: year of birth—2002. There is no information about education. In 2018, when Ezubchenko Jr. became the holder of a stake in the Cyprus Bank, the boy was 16 years old. He became deputy chief of staff to President Putin when he was twenty.

7

Freeport Vladivostok

No later than 2012, Rybolovlev told his partner Trutnev about the "Freeports." Rybolovlev's idea of Freeports went something like this: billions and billions of valuable works of art, precious stones, gold, diamonds, and even wine are in a small room, and you have the opportunity and administrative resources to build the same open port without competition on your territory, where you have complete control over customs, territory, and security—that is, everything. And this is a real jackpot.

Trutnev said "about Freeports" to Putin. Putin liked the idea and the "Freeport project" became the new and the most ambitious project of Rybolovlev-Trutnev-Putin. To be precise: Putin-Trutnev-Rybolovlev. It seems that all of Trutnev's upward hierarchical advancements since 2012 have been linked to the "Freeport project," which was decided to be built in Vladivostok. In May 2012 Trutnev was appointed as an assistant to President Putin. On August 31, 2013, Trutnev also became Deputy Prime Minister and an Authorized Representative of the President of Russia in the Far Eastern Federal District, where Rybolovlev and Trutnev were planning to create a Freeport (a tax-free trading harbor)—mainly for diamond trading, but also for trading in "everything"—gold, armaments—all bypassing Europe and US through Freeports in Asia. At least one Freeport in Asia (in Singapore) was already established by then[61].

Bouvier was already involved in serious business in Vladivostok. One of his Russian partners in a transport campaign was engaged in transporting diamonds for Alrosa through Vladivostok, which was gradually becoming the diamond center of Russia. The old Vladivostok airport was given over to this project, where buyers from India, for example, came to supervise the cutting of diamonds. Gradually, all these foreigners were pushed out of diamond mining and production, and only the interests of numerous Russian regional groups remained, and it was quite difficult to remove them from the diamond pipe. But none of this had anything to do with the Freeport. Selling diamonds from Vladivostok and the Freeport were two completely different projects. It's just that the location and the participants in these projects were largely the same.

On December 4, 2014, Putin proposed to grant Vladivostok the status of "a Freeport with attractive and favorable Customs regime."[62] This was a move aimed at reorienting Russian trade towards Asian markets. Freeport and the new trade direction, known as the "turn to the East", were designed to circumvent the US and EU financial sanctions imposed on Russia after the annexation of Crimea in March 2014.

On July 13, 2015, Putin signed into law the proposed legislature "Regarding Vladivostok as a Freeport" (No. 212-F3). It included a very important amendment that Rybolovlev insisted on (Article 30): "Storage on the territory of the Freeport of Vladivostok of certain types of especially valuable property, including luxury items, works of art, and antiques." It was primarily about storing Russian diamonds and gold in a Freeport and bartering them with buyers from Asia through Freeports to bypass the international banking system and Western sanctions. The law was ratified by the Russian Parliament on October 12, 2015, and went into effect.

Now with the ensuing madness, everyone wanted "in" on Trutnev-Rybolovlev's Freeport—including all of the Far-Eastern ports in Russia, the submarine base of the Pacific Fleet, the airport in Kamchatka. This is an excerpt from the Russian Wikipedia description of the Freeport in Vladivostok:

"Immediately after the law regarding Vladivostok as a Freeport went into effect, the expansion of the Freeport regime to the key ports in the Far East started being discussed. [...] Further, under the legislation, the Freeport regime could be extended to the submarine base of the Pacific Fleet in Viluchinsk and to the airport Elizovo in Kamchatka. The government of the Sakhalin Region proposed to include three seaports in Sakhalin into the Vladivostok Freeport regime project. In Khabarovsk Region, it was planned to include five seaports into the Freeport regime project, whereas in the

Chukotka Autonomous District—four seaports."[63]

In September 2015, the first meeting on this issue took place in Luxembourg between representatives of the Russian leadership and David Arendt, CEO of Le Freeport in Luxembourg, a company owned by Bouvier. To continue the conversation that had been initiated, on 6 November, Arendt was sent an official invitation to visit Moscow by the adviser to the Russian Minister for the Development of the Far East:

"Highly appreciating your experience and qualifications in managing the Freeport of Luxembourg, we invite you to discuss the possibility of developing a project similar to the "Freeport of Luxembourg" in the Russian Far East with Y.V. Trutnev, Deputy Prime Minister of the Russian Federation, Plenipotentiary Representative of the President of the Russian Federation in the Far Eastern Federal District, and A.S. Galushka, Minister of the Russian Federation for the Development of the Far East, from 9 to 13 November 2015 in Moscow. Given your busy schedule, if you are unable to visit us in Moscow on these dates, we would be grateful to receive your wishes on the date of your visit."

This is simply extraordinary. Since January 2015, Rybolovlev had initiated legal actions against Bouvier all around the world and had run an extraordinary effective black PR campaign to portray him as a bandit, and in September of the same year, Robolvovlev's friend, business partner and protector contacted Bouvier to propose him to do business together and build a freeport in Vladivostok.

The only rational explanation was that by September 2015, Trutnev understood that Rybolovlev's legal attempts to steal Bouvier's freeport in Singapore was failing, and therefore he needed now to negotiate with Bouvier to get his support to build the freeport in Vladivostok. This support Bouvier's claim that Rybolovlev was acting from the very beginning on behalf of the Kremlin to steal his freeport technology and know-how to build one in Vladivostok[64].

On 25 November, a Russian report on the outcome of another meeting between Galushka and Arendt in Luxembourg was published. "Such Freeports are very popular and have been established in Luxembourg, Switzerland and Singapore, with the Luxembourg experience considered the most successful." Galushka commented. "Luxembourg's Freeport is a successful world-class project worth €55 million."

On 31 December 2015, Evgenia Pershina, an official of the Russian state agency for foreign investment, sent Arendt an email on "Freeport of Vladivostok" informing Arendt that Trutnev and Galushka intended to make a business trip to Luxembourg on 22 or 23 January 2016. "Among other issues, they would like to discuss with you a place to store valuable cargo. But in order to choose a suitable land plot, we need to know your requirements for it. For example, the square footage of the leased land (its length and width), the amount of electricity, the depth—if you need a marine terminal, and so on," the letter stated.

The letter was accompanied by maps of Vladivostok detailing potential storage sites, including Cape Pospelov as the most suitable. "Once we receive these requirements from you, and if the area depicted in the attached files is suitable for your project, we will be able to find a suitable land plot for you," Pershina wrote.

However, the January meeting was cancelled at the last minute, formally due to snowfall. Instead of Trutnev and Galushka, only Dmitry Rogozin, Deputy Prime Minister of Russia, flew to Luxembourg on 22 January, having previously visited Monaco's Freeport with the Russian delegation.

Trutnev was scheduled to fly to Singapore on 29 April 2016, already without Galushka, to visit the Freeport of Bouvier and "present his Freeport of Vladivostok project". On 25 April 2016, Pershina sent an email to Arendt with the subject line "Vladivostok project" informing him that Albert Rakipov, Deputy Director of the Department of Foreign Economic Activity, Investment, Export Attraction and Support would be arriving in Singapore on 26 April for a three-day visit and would like to visit the same facilities and meet with the same companies as Trutnev did during his visit.

On 10 May 2016, Rakipov emailed six documents to Bouvier and his aides:

Dear Colleagues,

Following the agreement reached, I am sending to your attention a set of materials related to the meeting with DPM [Deputy Prime Minister] Yu. Trutnev.

1. general presentation [PowerPoint] on the Russian Government and measures for the development of the Far East.

2. General description [memorandum] on the Russian Government

and measures for the development of the Far East.

3. Infographics on special promising economic zones. 4.

4. Infographics on the Freeport.

5. Current preferences and benefits for residents of the Freeport of Vladivostok.

6. Frequently asked questions about the Freeport.

17 May Rakipov provided the management of the Singapore Freeport with the list of participants of the Singapore visit:

Yury Trutnev, Deputy Prime Minister of the Russian Federation, Plenipotentiary Representative of the President of the Russian Federation in the Far Eastern Federal District

Alexander Osipov[65], First Deputy Minister of the Russian Federation for the Development of the Far East

Alexei Chekunov, Director General of the Far East Development Fund

Vyacheslav Shport, Governor of Khabarovsk Krai

Pyotr Shelokhaev, Director General of the Far East Investment Attraction Agency

Alexei Tkachev, Assistant to the Deputy Prime Minister of the Russian Federation, Plenipotentiary Representative of the President of the Russian Federation in the Far Eastern Federal District

Timur Chernyshev, Assistant to the Deputy Prime Minister of the Russian Federation, Plenipotentiary Envoy of the President of the Russian Federation to the Far Eastern Federal District

Albert Rakipov, Deputy Director of the Ministry of the Russian Federation for the Development of the Far East

Andrey Zharkov, President of PJSC Alrosa

Daria Mandrova, interpreter

Rakipov also said that the delegation will include two or three more people and an unspecified number of press and media representatives. He added that he would call later to discuss the possibility of a photo shoot for Trutnev at the port. Russian Ambassador to Singapore Andrei Tatarinov was not included in the list as his presence was taken for granted.

The "unnamed" "two or three people" were FSB officers included in the delegation.

On 20 May 2016, Trutnev issued a statement from the Russian side about involving Bouvier and his company PSA in the construction of the Vladivostok Freeport "at all stages" of its development, "because we need to build ports, we need to manage ports" and in "this Singapore has accumulated" a lot of experience. The next day, Bouvier organized a tour for the Russian delegation of Singapore's Freeport.

"For them, they saw a big advantage in the fact that Vladivostok was close to Asia. They thought that this way they could increase trade with Asian countries. The Freeport was like a second parallel banking system for them. It was a big project, but I could easily realize it," Bouvier recalled.

The meeting started at 1 p.m. and lasted three hours. At one-point Trutnev asked everyone to leave, including the Russian ambassador. Only the interpreter, Trutnev, his two personal advisers (Alexander Osipov and Alexei Chekunkov[66]), Bouvier and Bouvier's lawyer remained in the room.

Bouvier prepared the cocktails; Trutnev began discussing the project to create a Freeport in Vladivostok. "When I raised the issue of a Freeport, everyone told me that I should meet and discuss this issue with you... I have heard so much about you in connection with Freeports," Trutnev said to Bouvier. He asked Bouvier to build a new Freeport in Vladivostok and invited him to come to Moscow to continue discussing the project. Bouvier replied that he was ready to consider such cooperation, but clarified: "As you know, I have had problems with one of your fellow citizens," without calling Rybolovlev by name. "Until this problem is resolved I will not go to Russia." "Don't worry," Trutnev replied. "As for this problem, I will take care of it."

However, no action was taken by Trutnev to resolve the conflict between Rybolovlev and Bouvier, at least with no consequences of this conversation.

During this meeting Trutnev told Bouvier that he pledged to Putin to create a Freeport in Vladivostok in 4-6 years: "I have instructions from the president, and I want to follow these instructions. There are specific deadlines and dates, and there is a plan to develop Vladivostok and the port. I am a responsible person. The President appointed me as this responsible person. And I need to make sure that this plan is implemented so that I can retire quietly," Trutnev said. "It wasn't about money," Bouvier commented on what Trutnev said, "it was about something more, that yes, he needs to do what the president has asked him to do so that he can then, roughly speaking, be left alone."

Trutnev said he was ready to give Bouvier the funding he needed to build the port. Bouvier, for his part, sent a group of engineers to Vladivostok to assess the situation on the spot, and on 22 June 2016 sent Trutnev a memo on possible cooperation in the creation of a Freeport in Vladivostok. However, against the backdrop of the conflict with Rybolovlev, and the conflict with Rybolovlev was not resolved despite Trutnev's promises, Bouvier decided not to participate in the Vladivostok project. He last visited Russia in 2013, even before the annexation of Crimea. After the start of the legal battle with Rybolovlev, it became unsafe for Bouvier to fly to Moscow. And without traveling to Russia, it was impossible to deal with the Vladivostok Freeport.

One of the questions the parties discussed in connection with the Freeport in Vladivostok was the question of using the ports for transportation and storage of Russian diamonds—primarily, along the Vladivostok-Singapore route, bartering them with buyers from Asia to bypass the international banking system and Western sanctions.

Putin's idea at the same time was to create a system through which he, through Trutnev, would control the entire supply chain for diamond production and trade, beginning with the extraction and ending with the sale to the end customer. Putin thought that by eliminating the middlemen, it would be possible to double the profit.

"Do we know the magnitude of the profit?" I asked Bouvier. "It should be easy to estimate," he replied. "One needs to look at the revenues and profits of Alrosa."

The profits appear impressive. According to Russia's Ministry of Finance, in 2008, the diamond mining volume in Russia was approximately 162,9 million carats with an estimated value of $12,7 billion. In 2009, it was less—about 120,2 million carats with an estimated value of $8,3 billion[67].

And if one adds to it the blood African diamonds "laundered" through Russia and Freeport in Vladivostok, en route to Singapore? And what if we add gold? And the weapons destined for the various sides in the numerous ongoing armed conflicts?

We know that diamonds have been the primary focus since Rybolovlev's diamond mining company Permgeologodobycha received its first extraction license in 2009 (Rybolovlev was involved in the diamond business since at least 2001). The license was issued for the development of the Rybyakov mine, which was estimated to hold approximately 127.800 karats. Rybolovlev subsequently obtained the second, and last, license in the Perm Region, thus monopolizing the regional diamond mining through becoming an owner of the only company, which held government licenses in the entire region.

Trutnev was also overseeing Alrosa, the diamond mining group of companies, that belonged to the Russian Government. He was trying for some years to replace its CEO Fedor Andreyev with his own man.

Indeed, there was enough to fight for: Alrosa mines approximately 95% of all of the diamonds mined in Russia and has a 25% share of the worldwide diamond mining volume. Alrosa is also estimated to account for one-third of the worldwide diamond stockpile.

Andreyev was summoned to Moscow for a "talk" in 2014. "I may have failed to introduce myself. My name is Yuri Trutnev, and I am the Deputy Prime Minister. I would like to remind you, that this is not your company but is a state enterprise." This was the opening line of Trutnev on that day.

Andreyev looked up from his mobile phone and replied to Putin's assistant: "We shall see."[68]

In September 2014, Andreyev was relieved of his post. In 2015, he died of cancer. On 23 April 2015, Andrey Zharkov who had attended a meeting with Bouvier in Singapore was installed as the CEO. On 16 November 2015, Oleg Petrov became the CEO of one of the group companies of Alrosa, Unified Sales Organization (USO).

Petrov was a graduate of the Military Institute of the Ministry of Defense of Russia and was previously employed as a Director of Sales and Marketing of Uralkali. The USO was responsible for sorting, appraising, presale, and sale-related activities in connection with the diamonds mined by other companies in the Alrosa Group. Petrov had a close relationship of trust with Rybolovlev and had attended his birthdays on several occasions. At the festive table, Rybolovlev paid the most attention to Petrov, which did not go unnoticed by the others present.

In other words, Trutnev and Rybolovlev succeeded in asserting control over the Russian diamond trade starting at the end of 2015. This colorful picture should be augmented by one more detail: on 13 March 2017, a new president of Alrosa was appointed. It was Sergei Ivanov Jr., the son of the former Head of President Putin's Administration and a KGB/FSB General Sergei Ivanov.

Freeport in Vladivostok was created, among other things, to trade in polished diamonds, to oust all intermediaries from the polished diamond market, for the *de facto* monopoly in this market by Alrosa, which pushed out numerous Russian governors who had diamond mines in Russia, which guaranteed them both money and influence. Now all these financial flows were channeled to Alrosa and Vladivostok, bypassing the regions.

Formally speaking, the Freeport was created. But it was not the Freeport that was meant and not the one that Trutnev promised to Putin. It was in Vladivostok that Russia was able to turn rough diamonds into polished diamonds and organize the export of Russian diamonds through Vladivostok. But storing these diamonds in the Freeport and conducting transactions not through the SWIFT banking system, using the capabilities of the Freeport: the structure, expertise, security, and trust required for "barter" transactions, when diamonds from the Freeport's storerooms without leaving any traces were exchanged by clients for gold, paintings or cash stored in the Freeport, was never realized. This required Bouvier with his unquestionable authority, reputation and the trust of clients.

8

The Hunt for Debtor Donald Trump

During Trump's 2016 presidential campaign, the press could barely keep up with Rybolovlev's flight routes to destinations where he turned up at the same time as Donald Trump or his family members. According to one of the newspapers, during 12 months, the private jet A-319 belonging to Rybolovlev with a number "M-KATE made at least seven visits to New York City (EWR), spending several days or more on each visit, usually overlapping with Trump presence there, given his habit of flying back most nights during the campaign. M-KATE made two 1-2-day trips to Miami when Trump was at Mar-a-Lago, the first at Thanksgiving. […] M-KATE also made 7 visits to Moscow (VKO) […]. This could be a coincidence, but the 12-month record shows clear patterns beyond a few simultaneous airport visits, easily able to support shuttle diplomacy."[69]

Rybolovlev himself insisted that he had never met Trump or had any dealings with anyone that was part of his campaign. Nevertheless, his jet and his yacht were spotted numerous times near Trump, his family members, one of Trump's financiers Robert Mercer, and one of Trump's attorneys, Michael Cohen. "According to his flight plans," wrote Bill Palmer, "Rybolovlev started in the Hamptons in early August" 2016 when Cohen was also in the Hamptons. "From there, Rybolovlev traveled to Dubrovnik, Croatia at a time when Ivanka Trump and Jared Kushner just happened to be vacationing in that same city."[70] Rybolovlev's yacht "My Anna" was spotted in Dubrovnik those days as well. At the same time, Rybolovlev maintained that he had never met Kushner.[71]

On 30 October, 2016, Rybolovlev set out after Trump in Las Vegas but came too late: his jet landed in Las Vegas 37 minutes after Trump's jet took off[72].

On 3 November 2016, Rybolovlev's jet was seen next to Trump's jet in Charlotte (North Carolina), where Trump conducted his Presidential campaign. In March 2017, Rybolovlev stated through his press secretary Chernitsyn that he and his plane were indeed at the airport in Charlotte at the same time as Trump but that it was purely coincidental. "Particular attention has been focused on a trip made by Mr. Rybolovlev to North Carolina," said Chernitsyn. "He was in North Carolina for a business meeting and we can state categorically that he did not have any contact with Mr. Trump or any of his advisers at the time he was there."

During the weekend of 11 February 2017, Rybolovlev's jet was seen in Miami when Trump was entertaining the Prime Minister of Japan at Mar-a-Lago. On 10-13 March 2017, Rybolovlev's yacht "My Anna" turned up near Robert Mercer's yacht "Sea Owl" which was anchored off the North Sound near Virgin Gorda, British Virgin Islands. According to the photographs and *Palm Beach Post*, the two yachts were "separated only by a few sailing vessels between them. The two vessels were a couple of hundred feet away from each other on Friday [10 March] and about 1000 feet apart as late as Monday [March 13], according to data from www.marinetraffic.com."

"Mr. Rybolovlev has never met Robert Mercer and has no relationship with him whatsoever," stated Rybolovlev's representative, Brian Cattell, on 14 March 2017.[73]

So, what happened in August 2016, and why did Rybolovlev start following Trump and his inner circle? Well, here is what happened: on 19 July 2016, Trump was nominated by the Republican Party as its Presidential candidate. Since that date, he became not just a businessman rescued from bankruptcy by Rybolovlev for unknown reasons back in 2008. Since 19 July 2016, Trump has been a (potentially) future President of the United States. Now it was a whole different ball game. Trump owed Rybolovlev, and the "original" $95 million was now worth significantly more. Trump knew this. Rybolovlev knew this. Trutnev knew this. General Ezubchenko knew this. And, of course, Putin knew this. Putin also knew that Trump owed him personally since not a single large financial investment into Trump from Russia, beginning with the period of 2007-2008, happened without Putin's knowledge, consent, and blessing.

So, Rybolovlev's jet was seen in North Carolina on 21 April and 3 November 2016, where, as it turned out, business meetings took place involving the leadership of the Swiss company Alevo and the leadership of its US affiliates, Alevo USA Inc. and Alevo Manufacturing Inc.

Alevo Group SA was established in Verbier, Switzerland, in 2009; it engaged in development of the energy storage systems employing GridBank technology. The company announced the construction of a high-tech factory for the production and manufacturing of batteries, and a planned investment of CHF 400-500 million into the business. Rybolovlev, who bought $35 million worth of shares in 2016, was the main shareholder of Alevo. Alevo's U.S. operations were primarily run by a company called Alevo USA Inc. which was bought back in 2014, before Rybolovlev became a shareholder, a former Philip Morris cigarette manufacturing plant in Concord, North Carolina, for $68,5 million for a new battery manufacturing location. On 3 November 2016, he made a strategic decision to transfer the production and manufacturing facilities to Concord, North Carolina, and transferred there three of his trusted managers—Kuzma Marchuk, a former Chief Financial Officer of Uralkali who took the company public and received a $12 million bonus; Elena Samsonova, a former Chief Human Resources Officer of Uralkali; and Mikhail Sazonov.

Alevo's arrival was announced in the local media with great enthusiasm. In 2016, Rybolovlev invested $126 million in Alevo's Swiss parent company. By October 2017, more than $200 million had already been invested. The investment was made through two Cyprus-registered trusts, Abalith Holdings Ltd and Gingerpath Ltd. Both trusts were registered in Cyprus under the address of Andreas Neocleous. Abalith was the sole shareholder of Gingerpath. Abalith's sole shareholder was Bolton Trustees, a holding company whose ultimate beneficial owner is Rybolovlev.

It was planned that the company could employ up to 2,500 people by 2017 and produce 16.000 batteries by 2019. However, these projections turned out to be utopian.

The business plan of Rybolovlev consisted of counting on the help of President Trump (who owed him) and of Wilbur Ross who was nominated by Trump to the post of US Secretary of Commerce on 30 November 2016, and confirmed as a US Secretary of Commerce in February 2017)[74] to obtain US Government contracts for Alevo.

"Let's say you're in Russia and you're producing new generators, and yet you are friends with the government. So, you're sure your generators will be bought everywhere," Bouvier reflected on Rybolovlev and his pursuit of Trump. "He thinks the same about America: If I'm friends with the president, with the "boss," then the "boss" will help me. And if he also owes me a favor, he'll help me all the more." "If he has an arrangement with the people around Trump, to have this kind of battery business is a fantastic business," one economist commented. "If you have government support and orders, every smallest place in America—hospital or small business— will buy it. You bring the business; we bring the orders."

In addition, Rybolovlev's company was hoping to get North Carolina State tax incentives. Indeed, Cabarrus County Commissioners and Concord City Council approved the package of tax incentives for Alevo totaling almost $10 million, while the North Carolina State Economic Investment Committee has voted to give Alevo more than $2,6 million in Job Development Investment Grants for expansion. In February 2017, after accepting $13,2 million in North Carolina state and local incentives, Alevo pledged to spend $251.5 million to build a new battery assembly line at its Concord plant and to add more than 200 jobs over the next five years, employing more than 500 people by 2022[75]. However, instead of the promised 500 employees, the company had only 140, and no additional investments were made. Unpaid contractors had filed $4,3 million in liens against the company, which asserted it would settle the claims with new financing. By March 2017, Alevo already had 215 employees and stated that it continued hiring for jobs in manufacturing, engineering, maintenance, logistics, and supply chain[76] in anticipation of the Government contracts.

In order not to bring attention to the connection between the anticipated US Government contracts for Alevo and Rybolovlev, who rescued Trump from bankruptcy and was a co-investor in the Bank of Cyprus with Wilbur Ross prior to his appointment as the US Secretary of Commerce, Rybolovlev's ownership of Alevo was kept secret from everyone, including North Carolina State officials. Robert Carney, executive director of Cabarrus Economic Development, said that they were unaware of Alevo's relationship with Rybolovlev. Beth Ann Gargan, of the North Carolina Commerce Department, also said the State never had any involvement or communication with Rybolovlev.

On 21 March 2017, about a month after it won the tax incentives from North Carolina, Alevo announced that it had appointed Vladislav Baumgertner as its new CEO[77]. In May 2017, another former Uralkali employee, Oleg Petrov, was appointed commercial director of Alevo Group[78].

However, neither Baumgertner's and Petrov's arrival nor the potential tax incentives managed to save Rybolovlev's company. In March 2017, it became known that Rybolovlev, who previously bought Trump's villa and who was now chasing Trump and his inner circle, was the owner of Alevo. Thus, the expectations of the lucrative Government contracts had to be abandoned. Indeed, being in the public eye and a focus of so much attention by Congress, neither Ross nor Trump could have anything to do with granting Government purchase orders to a company of the Russian oligarch Rybolovlev.

In August 2017, not having existed even a year under the new management, Alevo USA Inc. and Alevo Manufacturing Inc. declared bankruptcy and laid off their entire workforce (approximately 290 people by then). While Alevo was operating in the US, only one GridBank battery designed for storage of solar-generated power was launched in Hagerstown, Maryland. According to the bankruptcy filings made with a North Carolina bankruptcy court, Alevo USA Inc. and Alevo Manufacturing Inc. each had assets with a value "between $1 million and $10 million" and liabilities "between $10 million and $50 million."[79] Rybolovlev was not able to realize the return on his Trump investment through the Government purchase orders for Alevo.

It became necessary to look for other avenues for the return. They were soon found: Rybolovlev began acting through Arab sheikhs, which made sense since Trump's first foreign trip as a President was to Saudi Arabia on 20 May 2017[80]. At the end of October, Jared Kushner unexpectedly arrived in Saudi Arabia for a meeting with the Crown Prince. It is not clear what was discussed by Kushner and the Crown Prince bin Salman. But on November 4, a week after Kushner's return to Washington, the Crown Prince commenced his anti-corruption campaign, which included arrests of 200 members of the prince's family and their detention at the Ritz Carlton Riyad Hotel.

One can suppose that Kushner's visit to Saudi Arabia might somehow provoke the coup; that the coup was discussed with the government of the United Arab Emirates and that the support for the coup expressed by Trump via Twitter on November 6 was not coincidental. The coup might have been agreed upon among Abu Dhabi, the Crown Prince of Saudi Arabia Mohammad bin Salman and Trump. Could it be that in exchange, the two Arab governments would help Trump with a small and trivial matter— to settle finances with Rybolovlev, once and for all?

On 15 November 2017, the Crown Prince of Saudi Arabia began bidding on Christie's action through an intermediary for the painting depicting Jesus Christ which was attributed to Da Vinci.

The opening price of $100 million was increasing rapidly since the Crown Prince suddenly had an unknown and previously unidentified competitor. The bidding ended at $450,3 million. An unknown competitor who in the end lost out to the Crown Prince turned out to be the representative of the United Arab Emirates. Saudi Arabia and the UAE were bidding against each other for the painting, inflating the price to the necessary level. This was a thank-you gift from the Crown Prince to Trump for Washington's support of the coup in Saudi Arabia.

But in any special operation, there are missteps: unforeseen interference in the process of the "guarantee buyer" took $150 million out of Rybolovlev's pocket. Although until the very end, it was not clear exactly how much Rybolovlev would lose because of the existence of a buyer-guarantor: the existence of a buyer-guarantor auction must be announced in advance, but the amount guaranteed by this buyer until the end of the auction is kept secret.

Having prevailed in purchasing the painting over the UAE competitor, the Crown Prince presented it as a gift to the museum in the UAE. Abu Dhabi received the painting from the Crown Prince also as a thank-you for the support of the coup and for recognizing the Crown Prince as the new legitimate ruler of Saudi Arabia. And Rybolovlev, who made $125,5 million on the sale of the painting, an amount in all cases greater than the $95 million paid in 2008 for Trump's villa, finally stopped following Trump and his loved ones: after 15 November 2017, Rybolovlev's plane was never near Trump again. As someone who knows Ibn Salman said, when he buys something from someone, he understands that he is doing that person a favor.

In March 2018, when the Crown Prince paid a return visit to

Washington. The parties discussed arms purchases, as well as investments of hundreds of billions of dollars into the US economy[81]. Given the magnitude of these figures, the $450,3 million purchase price of the *Salvator Mundi* was a mere trifle, which could be easily incorporated into the overall negotiation pricing for government contracts for hundreds of billions of dollars between the new government of Saudi Arabia and the Trump Administration.

The sale of *Salvator Mundi* was not the only money laundering operation by Rybolovlev through his paintings. After the auction, Rybolovlev sold to the "Arab sheiks" additional paintings for about $300 million. Who were the buyers and which specific paintings were sold is not known. There is an assumption that these paintings were bought by Ibn Salman, maybe to compensate Rybolovlev for the loss of $150 million due to the buyer-guarantor.

The same group of "angel investors" who became suddenly enamored with Rybolovlev, offered to buy from him the Monaco Football Club for $500 million given that he encountered serious difficulties in Monaco: because of the corruption scandal,[82] he fell out of favor with Prince Albert and the latter refused to grant him citizenship, hinting that Rybolovlev should leave Monaco.

Rybolovlev then obtained Uruguayan citizenship (which does not recognize international extradition laws) and tried in 2019 to make his son-in-law Juan Sartori president of the country. However, Sartori did not become president of Uruguay, failing in the elections. Instead, he became the youngest senator of the Uruguayan Parliament.

9

Oleg Kalugin, ex-KGB General
ex-KGB head of Political Operations in the US

The year 2000 turned out to be a turning point in the lives of two previously little-known politicians: Vladimir Putin and Donald Trump. The first became president of Russia after manipulating the constitution and rigging elections. The latter lost the presidential race as the Reform Party candidate but forever marked himself as a contender for the presidency of the United States.

In 1999, the Kremlin was faced with the task of replacing President Boris Yeltsin with a suitable candidate. By then, the situation was tightly controlled by state security (GB), and the candidates proposed to Yeltsin were all from the GB: Yevgeny Primakov, former director of the Foreign Intelligence Service (SVR); Sergei Stepashin, former director of the Federal Counterintelligence Service (FSK—then the name of the future FSB); and, finally, Vladimir Putin, director of the FSB. Yeltsin could have chosen any one of the three—power was still in the hands of the FSB.

Yeltsin tried all of them, appointing them to test them as Prime Minister of Russia. According to the Russian constitution, in case of death or resignation of the president, it was the prime minister who took the place of the departed one as acting president of Russia. The acting president was then easily put through elections because it was assumed that in a country like Russia, which before 1991 knew neither free elections nor democracy, an acting president appointed by the Kremlin would not meet serious opposition from the country's regional leaders and the people.

Yeltsin was disappointed with Primakov and Stepashin: they were successively appointed and removed as prime minister in the same year, 1999.

On 9 August 1999, Putin was appointed prime minister. On 31 December 1999, Yeltsin resigned before the end of his term, making Putin acting president. On 26 March 2000, having previously started the second Chechen war, Putin won the election in the first round, receiving 53% of the popular vote, with the required minimum of 50% plus 1 vote.

Meanwhile, in January 2000, New York real estate mogul Donald Trump announced his candidacy for the Reform Party presidential nomination, meaning he essentially became an independent candidate who did not represent the major US political parties, Republican and Democratic. On 14 February, Trump officially ended his campaign: a poll comparing Trump to likely Republican nominee George W. Bush Jr. and likely Democratic nominee Al Gore showed that Trump would have received the support of 7% of voters. In August 2001, Trump switched to the Democratic Party, calculating his chances of winning as the now Democratic nominee, but never decided to enter the race.

But even though Trump lost the 2000 campaign, Moscow, where the equally unknown "Who is Mr. Putin?" had just won the election, could not ignore the ambitious playboy Donald Trump, whose girlfriends were porn stars and whose wives were girls from modeling agencies. All the more so because Trump had been on the radar of the Russian intelligence services since his first trips to the USSR in the 1970s. Now, in 2000, former FSB Director Vladimir Putin became the Russian president.

My 70-minute conversation with former KGB general Oleg Kalugin took place on 31 March 2019 at his home in Washington, DC. The conversation was recorded on a tape recorder, which was quite atypical for Kalugin to allow. During the entire recording, he looked at this tape recorder with a burning light bulb very distrustfully, as if there was a cobra on the coffee table in front of him.

I was trying to pose short, "black-and-white" questions hoping to receive simple answers. I cannot say that I succeeded, as by the end of my interview, I could not help but feel that General Kalugin's answers to some of my questions were deliberately equivocal.

I then decided to involve Vladimir Popov, former KGB Lieutenant Colonel, who was my co-author of the books *The Corporation: Russia and the KGB in the Age of President Putin* (2008), *The KGB Plays Chess* (2010), and *From Red Terror to Terrorist State: Russia's Intelligence Services and their Fight for World*

Domination, 1917-2036 (2023), and who is political exile living in Canada. During his service at the KGB, he specialized in recruiting agents from the population of athletes and intellectuals—writers, journalists, and actors. I asked Mr. Popov to evaluate the information supplied by his former colleague from a professional point of view. His commentary clarified several points in Kalugin's narrative and became an afterword of sorts to the interview itself.

Oleg Danilovich [Kalugin], you promised to discuss Trump with me. You said that you knew and appreciated the extent of Trump's activities in Moscow. Also, now that the Mueller investigation is over, I would like to know what you think about Trump.

Trump was elected by the American people, so here you must accept it—whether you like it or not…

Accepted.

But, for, example, during the prior Administration, I rather liked Obama for many reasons, but Trump, when he was still in Russia and long before he became a politician, behaved in a way that, let's just say, KGB took notice.

Could you please be more specific?

I do not recall whether he was married or not at the time, but he behaved rather freely.

Are we talking about 2013 or an earlier period?

It was before, since in 2013 I was already in the United States, and what I read in Russia, that was before 2000.

What do you mean by "read"?

There were some documents. As you know, there was a time when I had complete access to all the documents of that certain organization. I mean, that was before the collapse of the Soviet Union.

These were internal documents?

Yes, of course. At that time, all foreign visitors—especially those who expressed specific interest in Russian everyday life—e.g., girls and the like— were always noted and observed, as they say, with great interest.

Let's begin there since Putin recently gave a speech, and when…

Yes, my former subordinate.

And when he was asked about Trump, he said "You think we monitor all foreign visitors?"

Of course, not all foreign visitors are monitored—there are not enough resources for that physically—but the majority, especially those from the United States and Europe, were always monitored. KGB was the largest organization worldwide by the number of people, by the financing it received, and by other measurements. And, by the way, by the number of foreign agents. I can quote one specific figure—until 1962, I think, the Soviet intelligence had several hundred Americans in the States who were working for them. They mainly worked for the Soviets out of ideological convictions. […]

So, the idea that Trump was being watched by the Soviet intelligence forces, is correct?

Trump is a businessman who is rather successful as the scale of his operations shows, but when he was in Moscow, he met there with some Soviet female comrades, as they say, and must have left some mark.

He started visiting Moscow in the 1970s…

Yes, he started a while ago…

And he was watched by the KGB?

Certainly…

Because he was seeing some girls?

Yes.

How do you know that?

I know that since I still worked for the KGB.

So, it was in some internal memoranda?

Yes, since I was the Head of the Department of Foreign Counter-Intelligence Service. Its first mission was infiltration of all the foreign special service operations: intelligence, counter-intelligence, and police forces all over the world. But the United States, of course, was leading the pack, with NATO and European countries being second, et cetera. China was not prominent in that space back then.

And you remember Trump?

Yes, I remember. It was a long time ago and he was noted even back then.

If it were still during the 1980s, this information must relate to the period when Trump was visiting…

The Soviet Union still existed… Before the collapse, before the "geopolitical catastrophe", as Putin referred to it, the largest one in geopolitical terms…

Yes, "the largest geopolitical catastrophe in the world." Does this mean that Trump could have been recruited even back then?

No, it does not mean that he could have been recruited. But KGB for sure had a dossier on him.

What would typically happen in those circumstances?

It could be that nothing would happen, at least during that period. But at some later point in history or life, someone could have "remembered" about it. KGB generally had a pretty good "memory".

They could "remember" or would have "remembered" for sure?

They could. Not for certain, but they could.

What would need to happen for them to be certain to "remember"?

Well, if he were, for example, close to some Russia-related affairs, then [they would have "remembered"] certainly. But if he were somewhere in the periphery…

He did become close to Russia-related affairs. He conducted business, including business in Russia…

That is why he was of interest even before, in the old days. And, by the way, you know, he is rather friendly towards Putin, and I think it makes sense.

Yes, and we are trying to determine why is he so predisposed towards Putin.

I think it is partly because of that—what I am talking about.

Because he knows that there is some compromising information about him?

Yes, he knows.

And how is this compromising information captured? Videos? Testimony? Witness testimony?

I do not know.

There is information out there that Trump's first wife was being watched by the Czech Secret Service.

It is entirely possible. But if she were being watched by the Czech Secret Service, then she was also watched by the Soviet Secret Service. Because Czech intelligence and counter-intelligence were some of the closest to the Soviets, unlike, say Polish or Hungarian. The Czechs were our "brothers in arms" in all respects, at least until the Czech events, the Prague Spring [of 1968].

This happened later, in the 1970s.

But everything was fine during the 1970s. Everything was fine until the Soviet Union fell apart. Well, "normal" in terms of relations. Except… Well, the Poles were always rather self-reliant and that is understandable. The Hungarians at some point… The nicest and most reliable folks were certainly the Bulgarians.

Can you please tell me if it is indeed the case that Trump was watched by the Russian Intelligence?

It was inevitable for any American during that time.

If, as you said, there were compromising materials concerning him…

One can only guess.

You just said that he was into some "monkey business…"

Yes, just like many Americans. I read archive materials. By the way, it was already in Leningrad, when I was working as the First Deputy of the Head of the Leningrad KGB and had unlimited informational access, including access to different historical documents. And it was in Leningrad, since it was as important of capital as Moscow, that I happened to read a lot of rather interesting materials, including those about the United States, and Great Britain, of course.

And what was specifically described there, do you remember?

I do not remember, some meetings with women… It was typical for the American visitors…

And were these women random or were they "assigned" to him?

They could have been random, but the predominant majority of those "random" women who worked (i.e., slept) with the foreigners, were controlled by the KGB. There were certainly volunteers… But sooner or later, they all became informants. They were either punished for prostitution or had to work as informants.

So, we should not be imagining that there was pure love?

I do not think we should. I mean, everything is possible in this world.

And the modeling agencies from which many of these women originated, the modeling agencies themselves, were they all also watched by the Secret Service?

Yes—particularly within the Secret Service. The Internal Security Service. You know, during our time, they controlled everything except the Party organization. This was the only thing they could not do.

I ask because two wives of Trump, by some coincidence, are from the modeling agencies.

Yes, and in addition, both were, as they say, of Slavic descent.

So, is it too crazy to suspect that they could have been recruited before meeting Trump?

One cannot rule it out completely. I am not sure but cannot rule it out.

OK, so this person about whom there is compromising information and about whom it is known that he visited Russia, hooked up with women, becomes a Presidential candidate—still, just a candidate—from the Republican Party. What would you say should have been happening at that point in Moscow, on Lubyanka, former KGB, now FSB Headquarters?

No one would have objected in Moscow. On the contrary… They surely did not need Hillary Clinton. And her opponent, Republican, as a President—that would have been quite feasible for them.

So, the hypothesis that Moscow helped Trump during the Presidential Election campaign is correct?

One can suppose that this is the case, but I do not have any specific information. But I think it's possible.

And can one also suppose that Moscow was watching all this from the sidelines while knowing about Trump and the compromising information that exists about him, and did nothing?

It's possible… Let them elect, and then we can decide, after the election.

So, you presume that Moscow did not influence the election?

I think, they did not influence it in the sense that they did not undertake any specific action but the candidate himself thought that Moscow could influence the elections because one can expect from Moscow anything at any time. Be it Polonium or anything else.

So, it was a silent pact, or were there any specific actions?

I do not know. I would think it's possible that some actions took place, but I do not know. But the fact that the current President is friendly towards the Russian leader, is one of the indicators, in my opinion, that makes one think: "Why are they so friendly?"

The other day, we were all (or at least I was) surprised by the results of the Mueller investigation regarding the absence of proven collusion between the Trump Campaign and the Russian Government. What do you think about it?

They did not necessarily have to find something—the KGB was always successful at that.

And what were they looking for and what could they find?

Perhaps there were some materials. Because there were some defectors from the Soviet Union and people who left with documents. Like Litvinenko. By the way, when he lived in London and started talking about

Putin—he knew Putin personally—I called him and said, "Sasha, you should not be sharing these things with the press, you may have problems." And he died six months later. As unfortunate as it was, it's a fact. He, particularly, was blabbering away on topics that were not safe to blabber on, and he got Polonium. He was not the only one, but since he happened to live in London, the story became quite public… […]

There was a diplomat named Yevgeny Nikolayevich Makeyev. He worked in New York from 1971 to 1980 in a rather high post. I know that it is an atypically long term—nine years.

Agree, that it is not typical for the employees of the Ministry of Foreign Affairs.

Precisely. And at some point, he was something like a Deputy General Commissioner of the United Nations. But my question is this: I know that the diplomates resided in a special area designated for the diplomates.

Yes.

While he resided in a separate high-end skyscraper…

Yes, this is also telling.

Still, close to the UN, about two blocks away. And Trump lived in that same building during those years.

I think I read it somewhere.

Do you think it is a coincidence?

I am not sure. It might be.

Or maybe not?

Maybe not. I just do not know but I think either is possible.

And could it have been that starting as early as the 1970s, while Trump was not yet…

Not yet a political force…

But he was already recruited?

It is quite possible. By the way, when I was recruiting informants, my targets included Americans who at the time did not have much by way of access but could get it in time.

This coincides with the time when he met his first wife—i.e., it is in the 1970s.

It is quite possible. I cannot say for sure since I do not know. But it is possible because, during my last years at the KGB, I oversaw international operations around the world. For example, I had—well, not I, but in KGB where I worked—there was one of the leaders of the Australian intelligence. Australia is far away. But Australia is a member of the alliance: USA, Great Britain, New Zealand, Australia... He had document access of a scale that was unbelievable—such as to the UK documents. He delivered those to us. I traveled to Australia to meet with him.

If we suppose that there were some compromising materials regarding Trump...

Yes, it is quite possible.

What would a person like that be afraid of? What is Trump afraid of? Is he afraid of the publication coming out and describing how he took women to hotels in the 1970s?

I think that any reasonable person who is concerned about his career and personal life would not want this kind of publication wherever it was and whenever it was.

And that would be enough to be so explicit in expressing love and respect for Putin?

Yes. I think that this is one of the reasons for his friendly predisposition towards some of the Russian leaders.

You think that this reason is enough or maybe there is something else?

There may be something else too. But this is one of the serious reasons. By the way, when I worked in that organization, I had my approach to these types of issues. If someone caught me somewhere in bed with a woman and tried to recruit me, I would say to that person: "Listen, these pictures are so interesting, can you please make me a few copies for my friends?" This kind of reaction immediately changes the dynamic. You are showing that you do not care. This is how I would have acted. I am not kidding. [...]

What exactly is a "recruited foreign citizen"? What is the difference between that person and an unrecruited foreign one?

A recruited foreign citizen or any person is the person who acts following the requests or asks of the agent who recruited him.

How does the process of recruiting happen? Is it something formal? Is it a signed document? Is it just based on a promise?

There could be a signed document but not necessarily. Sometimes it is not necessary. For example, I recruited a few Americans. I never requested any sort of formal pronouncement from them along the lines of "I will work for you." For example, the first person whom I recruited—it was probably by pure chance. I was a student at Columbia University then. It was in 1958. In 1956 Nikita Khrushchev already gave his speech condemning the "crimes of Stalin". [...]

Oleg Danilovich, was Trump watched by the Russian intelligence?

He was.

So, for some time, he was being watched by the Russian intelligence.

As were all the Americans and foreigners.

And so, if the goal was to recruit him, how would it have been done? Someone comes to him and recruits?

Usually these are the people who have an opportunity to meet him informally, somewhere in private. There are ways and means for that. In a private setting, he could be told something or reminded of something.

How is he reminded: "Mr. Trump, we have some compromising materials on you?"

No, that would be too rude and obvious…. One should say: "We have not been in touch with you for a while, you are remembered well." To hint that there are some materials regarding him—he would understand that. There would be no direct attempt to blackmail—I never went about like that.

At that point, Trump is just another rich person. What makes him interesting?

Another rich person… I knew, for example, a person who became a friend of mine—he died a week ago at the age of 98. I have his picture on my wall, together with the former Head of the CIA, Colby. He was a billionaire. He said to me once: "Oleg, I would do anything for you." He was not interested in money, just in kinship.

Out of the pure friendliness?

Yes, out of the pure friendliness. By the way, I was told by another friend of mine (I think I can now talk about it—not sure that I ever spoke about this publicly), one of the FBI operatives, let's say, whose focus was Soviet affairs, that, Oleg, if I knew you before, I would have worked for you. I was at his funeral when he was being buried…

He meant that he would have become a Soviet spy?

I think so. Out of pure friendliness. As for the blackmail—I never engaged in it myself.

OK, let's say no one blackmailed Trump.

He could have been blackmailed… But it is unlikely in a given situation… He could have just been "reminded". And this immediately puts a person on guard and makes him want to resolve this peacefully without a scandal.

But what could one want from him? He was just a rich person at the time. Dealing in real estate...

A rich person is an investment into the Russian economy, or in a Soviet economy, and not directly but through some sort of an organization, which is a front and which KGB could create artificially—or through an already existing organization of that kind.

They want money from him or they are trying to pay him?

To pay him if need be. But the most important thing that is needed from him is information, not money. Russia always had the money.

What kind of information could Trump provide as a businessman?

He had connections with some bureaucrats. It could be that he understood the real economic situation in the country better than, say, some others.

So, he could be a source of information.

Yes, a source of information.

Not necessarily of the secret information?

Correct. I had a person like that, a Ph.D. in Political Science. He was about 15 years older than I. He was a lonely person—did not have women or friends. When I met him randomly, I realized that he was very educated and knew a lot. I decided to befriend him and to solve his issues. And so, after we met a couple of times, he told me: "Listen, Oleg, you are a discovery in my life. I would do anything for you." I said: "Please send me the analysis of the situation. I would be very grateful since they would appreciate it in Moscow and it would be gratifying for you." And he said: "Oleg, I would do it for you."

And what was that?

It was his analysis based on his knowledge of a given topic.

Was it attributed to him?

No, it's never done this way, and no one ever signs something like that.

That is, this was an anonymous document?

Absolutely. It was a revelation for me that he began to cooperate.

Can we suppose, for example, that if certain information was expected from Trump, that he, too, was asked to write something down?

It may be but is not necessarily so. Once could provide the documents too.

If there is a person like Trump who provides information, then there might be some permanent individual from the KGB in the US with whom he is in constant contact and who is being "kept" in America just for that purpose.

Yes, of course, it might be.

Is it possible that Makeyev was kept in the US because Trump lived in the same building with him?

One cannot rule it out, but one should not assert that without any evidence. It cannot be ruled out because intelligence is an intricate business. There are different nuances.

Do you have any individuals that you recruited in the US who only talk to you or do you, in reality, "pass them along" to anyone?

They talk only to me at some point but later, when I leave, when everything is over, or when I go on vacation for a couple of months...

Could they wait for a couple of months?

We had a person who worked at the National Security Agency at some point... I was then a Deputy Resident in Washington, an acting Resident. So, this person worked irrespective of anything. First, there is a system of communication involving secret places: information is deposited in a certain place. I succeeded in implementing that system. I met this one guy only once in my life, but I got very valuable documents from him when I worked here. He left them in a park, behind a stone. He drew me to the location of that secret spot. I checked it out. And I left money for him in the same spot—a thousand or however many dollars, depending on the circumstances.

So, if a person is recruited, he is being "curated" by only one person?

Yes. By the way, the KGB had, in that sense, a very strict code of retaining the source of information.

For how many years could this person curate an agent and stay in the US for that reason?

I told you a story about a person, whom I "led" for several years, and then he was "made" by one of our defectors who did not know either his last name or his first name but he relayed the information that the person transferred and he became a focus of investigation—they started to check and saw that he had a lot of money for some reason and he traveled a lot for some reason.... He went to Moscow then. And he was put in prison because Kryuchkov considered him a double agent. So, in intelligence, people's fates are very uncertain. I got lucky that Andropov believed me because otherwise, Kryuchkov would have put me in jail or would have arranged for some automobile accident, as it happened. That was the situation.

What is your impression of Trump after the two years?

It is obvious that he is trying to find some common ground with Putin. That much is clear.

Do you have any explanation for that?

I have one theory, which I already mentioned: when he was in Moscow back in the day, he could have left a "mark", and naturally, someone made use of it. Since his friendliness towards the current Russian government is somewhat unusual, I would say, for an American President. Somewhat unusual, indeed, and too heartily warm.

So, we can suppose, and really, this was done already multiple times, that there is compromising material concerning Trump.

I know for sure that there was compromising material. But I do not know whether it was used.

Is there anything in Trump's actions that would point not only to the existence of compromising material but to having been recruited?

His friendliness towards the current Russian government raises questions, of course.

In your opinion, as a person who worked for the KGB your whole life, is this the behavior of a person who knows that there is compromising material on him along the lines of the girls with whom he slept, or is this the behavior of a person who is a recruited agent?

It could be either of these. He might not have been recruited and he might be simply afraid. And this is being used as a reason, as a factor. If there was an attempt like that, it would have been a long time ago. And at that time, there would have been reasons for that.

For recruitment?

For being approached with an offer of recruitment. There is a common word—blackmail. But I already said that I, for once, would have never been influenced by blackmail. But this depends on a person's personality and the level of preparedness.

At what level are the people who have information regarding "Trump in Moscow"?

These are the people at a very high level. This is because all this happened a long time ago, and the documents are kept in special archives that cannot be accessed by a random employee who wants to find out something. [...]

Several attempts were made—one through Michael Flynn and Jared Kushner when they spoke to Sergei Kislyak in the Russian Embassy, and then, later, when Trump became President—there were several open attempts by Trump himself to speak with Putin one-on-one, without any US diplomats being present, what does it all tell you? This attempt was first made in Finland, then in Vietnam...

Yes, it all kind of took off from there...

What did they have to discuss with Putin one-on-one?

It was to establish a relationship of a kind that he would not feel like a potential blackmail victim. Because some time ago...

Trump?

Yes.

Trump was supposed to whisper something to Putin and to agree on something with him?

Of course, it was meaningful. About how "we will behave in a friendly manner, all of the differences in our systems and beliefs notwithstanding, and that we would remain true friends in a personal sense." And in that situation, Putin's behavior was entirely correct.

So, you think that the attempts to speak one-on-one might be rooted in the fact that there is some compromising material regarding Trump?

Not necessary. There might be other reasons, like getting to know a person in a real sense, as opposed to believing what you are being told.

But for that, he can meet with Putin in the presence of the American translator and the Secretary of State.

Yes, I understand. There are some reasons for that. But what these reasons are—one can only guess.

And what should we guess?

We could guess that this is connected to his presence in Moscow a long time ago. I think that this is connected to his Moscow experience. But this is my opinion.

Fine. So, we have been observing Trump for two years at this point. In your opinion, is he an agent or not?

I am not sure, I cannot say. But the fact that he left a trace in the KGB documents at that earlier time—this is certain. I do not have any doubts about that.

Do you remember what it was? Was it a one-page report, or was it a large volume?

In the USSR, a department called the 7th Directorate existed within the

KGB. This was a department that executed a physical surveillance and then they wrote reports about who communicated with whom and went where. And then the operatives analyzed what this could mean based on the existing materials—i.e., was it a random occurrence or if there was any meaning to it.

It was a known fact that hundreds, if not thousands, of Americans, used the services of the Russian girls, streetwalkers. And, of course, Soviet and Russian intelligence who were familiar with this situation, could use these girls in a specific way to make them earn money as they normally would, but also to earn something extra. Plus, there would be a guarantee that they would not be arrested for prostitution.

Did any US journalist call you with questions about Trump?

We talked but I never went into any detail… I am just speaking so openly with you, Yuri. No, I am always more careful with the Americans. By "careful", I mean "restrained".

But it's not like everyone was bothering you with questions about Trump…

Sometimes they tried, but I found ways to avoid answering. I am just speaking with you this way… Such is life. So, should we have a drink?

With pleasure. Many thanks.

Thus ended my conversation with Oleg Kalugin. I think it was the last interview he ever gave. I can't say that I was satisfied with what I heard. I found Kalugin's answers evasive and even contradictory. His numerous "it cannot be ruled out, but it cannot be asserted as well" seemed to me more like an evasion from a direct answer. The mention of Litvinenko, who was killed because he "talked about something he shouldn't have talked about and got polonium", did not seem to me to be accidental. It was as if Kalugin was constantly self-censoring, assessing what he was allowed to say about Trump and what he wasn't.

So, I turned for help to my co-author Vladimir Popov, a former KGB lieutenant colonel living in Canada. His specialty during his years of service in the 5th KGB Directorate was, among other things, recruiting agents from athletes and creative intellectuals—writers, journalists, and actors. I asked Popov to make an expert assessment of the information received from his former colleague. This comment clarified a lot of things in Kalugin's story and became a kind of afterword to my interview with Kalugin.

Your question is rather complex. It is complex because this topic if you will, is a lecture about how a secret service of any country operates. You may be surprised but nothing that Kalugin said in this interview seemed controversial to me. On the contrary, he appears as a typical intelligence officer with an extensive experience in Intelligence. For that type of person, it is sometimes more important to remain silent or to speak generally and indirectly, so that, as they used to say in the KGB, it would not be possible to hold you to your words later. It is due to that experience that he spoke to you in allegories. It is not at all random (as a rule, the most important points are made at the end of the conversation or a letter), that he emphasized that he is even more careful with the Americans. I am sure he was completely honest.

Now, I can speak briefly about the process of recruiting by the Secret Service, and then about Trump, a topic of interest to you.

Each recruiting process is unlike the other. There are always different triggering motives regarding an agreement to cooperate with the secret service, especially, with the secret service of another country. And really, the psychological contact of the secret service operative with a potential recruitment target is extremely important, irrespective of whether they are both citizens of the same country or different countries.

Whether a recruiting target signs something at the time of being recruited (using the KGB terminology) about cooperation or not, really depends on the preceding circumstances. As a rule, a written confirmation regarding an agreement was required when recruitment was based on some compromising materials. It is done just in case there is a later refusal to cooperate, as one more tool for blackmail.

Any extraordinary foreigner who entered the USSR and Russia today would have been and is now being, watched by the Soviet-Russian secret service. Observation begins at the moment the person applies for a visa at a consulate. That is why Foreign Intelligence officers serve as vice-consuls, or often even as consuls. From the moment that a foreign citizen applies for a visa, the first thing that happens is that there is a confirmation whether or not there is any information about him in an appropriate secret service department, after which there is an inquiry made at the Headquarters regarding any materials regarding that person and a recommendation about further investigation to the extent there is some information about him, such as regarding his position in a society (as a politician, a businessman, a journalist, et cetera).

Regarding Trump personally, I can state with full confidence that during his trips to the USSR and Russia, he was closely investigated by the local Secret Service. That kind of investigation was not conducted to recruit immediately. For the Secret Service, it was important to identify the psychological profile of a person, his political orientation, his attitude towards his home country and towards the country he was visiting for some reason. And then, after accumulating a sizable amount of material (based on a whole array of undertakings: plain observation, audio- and video-surveillance of the places of residence, agency-level scrutiny, including "honey traps"), based on the analysis, a decision is made about a transforming the investigation into recruitment with appropriate conditions (such as through compromising materials or a voluntary agreement) or about wrapping up the whole thing by "educating" a foreigner to convey a favorable image of a country that investigated him, in his home country.

There is a high probability that Trump was recruited in the USSR or in Russia since during his visits, he behaved rather carelessly. However, the only way to confirm that theory is by having access to his dossier, which the Russian secret service certainly has.

Trump's desire to meet with Putin one-on-one might be explained by him wanting to tell his vis-à-vis that his anti-Russian stance is nothing more but a condition of him remaining the President of the United States.

Once again about recruitment. The very fact that a foreign national realizes that he is in contact with an intelligence representative of another country and gives him some information, even verbally, is already considered an act of recruitment. Such an option concerning Trump seems to be quite admissible.

Epilogue

In Rybolovlev's camp, investigations and trials have become an ongoing phenomenon. In February 2017, a Nicosia court investigated Erotokritou, Panayiotis Neocleous and Neocleous & Co LLC on suspicion of abuse of power and corruption. Erotokritou was found guilty of corruption, bribery, abuse of power and conspiracy. Neocleous and his law firm were found guilty of conspiracy, corruption and bribery.

On 14 September 2017, *Le Monde* reported on a DVD with data extracted from Bersheda's phone. Hours after the publication, Narmino—Monaco's justice minister since January 2006—resigned.

On 22 September 2017, Judge Edouard Levraurt, on behalf of the Monaco Attorney General's Office, announced the opening of a judicial investigation against Rybolovlev, Bersheda and several high-ranking officials on charges of active and passive influence peddling and corruption in connection with Bouvier's arrest. Narmino was arrested the same day. Narmino's wife Christine and son Antoine were charged with conspiracy. Paul Masseron, interior minister from April 2006 to April 2015 was charged with passive influence peddling and breach of professional secrecy. Jean-Pierre Dréno, Attorney General of Monaco between May 2011 and September 2015, was charged for acts of criminal conspiracy with Rybolovlev and complicity in violating the right to private and family life. He was convicted on 8 June 2018[83].

Régis Asso, Principality Police Chief from April 2013 to February 2016 was accused of breach of professional secrecy. Christophe Haget, head of the judicial police until 2017—accused of passive influence peddling and corruption, as well as breach of professional secrecy. Frederic Fusari, chief of police until 2017, Haget's deputy—charged with passive influence peddling, corruption and breach of professional secrecy. The charges were also brought against Bernard Squarcini, director of France's Directorate General of Internal Security (DGSI).

Bersheda then appealed to the Swiss Supreme Court and demanded that the acquisition and use of data from her personal phone be recognized as unlawful. In September 2018 the court rejected her petition. But in the same September, the Geneva case against Rybolovlev and Bersheda was closed, as under Swiss law the offence must have actually been committed. Conspiracy to bribe a judge, if no bribe was paid, was not an offence under Swiss law: "While attempted extortion or bribery is an offence punishable by law, mere preparation to commit explicit extortion or bribery is not punishable," the prosecutor's report said, but stressed that attempted bribery was "ethically unacceptable and shocking" and that Tetiana Bersheda's actions were contrary to the rules of the legal profession. The case was then referred to the Geneva Bar Association to deal with Bersheda as they saw fit.

An investigation in Monaco has begun. On 6 November 2018, Rybolovlev was taken into custody and his house was searched. The following day, the Monaco prosecutor opened a judicial investigation against Rybolovlev and Bersheda on charges of corruption, influence peddling, violation of judicial processes and violation of privacy. Rybolovlev himself was accused of bribing and conspiring with Monegasque authorities to arrest Bouvier in Monaco in February 2015. Similar charges were brought against Rybolovlev in Cyprus.

In June 2019, Bouvier filed a criminal complaint against Rybolovlev in Paris for using and corrupting the French police and judicial system and directing police investigations against Bouvier in France and Monaco by organizing the illegal exchange of information with officials who came under Rybolovlev's influence.

In April 2021, the Swiss federal authorities in Bern initiated criminal proceedings against Rybolovlev and Bersheda, charging them under Article 271 of the Swiss Criminal Code for illegally luring Bouvier to Monaco, where they organized his arrest, as Switzerland has a law prohibiting the organization of provocations against Swiss citizens abroad. The peculiarity of this case was that the victim of the criminals was not Bouvier, but the Swiss Confederation, whose laws were violated.

Another case against Rybolovlev on charges of corruption and abuse of influence was opened in Paris. Two court cases against Rybolovlev were opened in Monaco on the Rappo lawsuit. As the court systems of Monaco and France are interconnected, losing the case in Monaco threatened Rybolovlev with a ban from the French Côte d'Azur.

Over the years, Rybolovlev, for his part, has filed eleven lawsuits against Bouvier: in Monaco, Singapore, Luxembourg, England, America, Liechtenstein, France and Switzerland. Nine of these eleven cases were won by Bouvier. Two cases remained open until recently. One was in Paris, which progressed very slowly because of the peculiarities of the French judicial system. The second was in Switzerland, where the prosecutor had already decided to close the case, but Rybolovlev appealed, and on 26 July 2022 the Court of Appeal reversed the previous decision and referred the case to the prosecutor's office to reopen the investigation. Following this decision, the prosecutor's office held several hearings that yielded no results that allowed charges to be brought against Bouvier.

At the end of May 2018, the New York prosecutor's office, after a year-long trial, rejected all charges brought by Rybolovlev against Bouvier and decided to dismiss the case in New York,[84] finding no basis to consider the resale of the paintings as fraud. Somewhat earlier, the court case against Bouvier was refused to be heard by a Singapore court.

On 12 December 2019, the Monaco Court of Appeal granted Bouvier's request to drop all criminal charges brought against him in Monaco due to the lack of judicial impartiality revealed in the investigation against Bersheda and Rybolovlev. The appeal judge in Monaco stated that "all the investigations [against Bouvier] were conducted in a biased and unfair manner, and the defendant has not had the opportunity to correct these serious anomalies that have permanently upset the balance of the parties' rights." In July 2020, the High Court of Justice of Monaco confirmed this decision and quashed all investigations against Bouvier because they were found to be "biased."

When asked why Rybolovlev did not end all these cases with peace agreements, Bouvier replied:

"When a billionaire walks into an art gallery—you don't want him to walk out of there. And when a billionaire walks into a lawyer's office—they don't want him to come out of there either. None of Rybolovlev's lawyers are interested in stopping milking this cow. In Geneva, for example, he is the law firm's biggest client. And if Rybolovlev stops working with them, they would lose serious money. In America, in New York, he is working with several law firms... Everyone knows that in New York, after the financial industry, the law firm industry is the most profitable."

As the years passed, and with the successful auction of the painting *Salvator Mundi*, the main accusation made by Rybolovlev against Bouvier fell away: Rybolovlev made money on the sold paintings acquired through Bouvier, not lost it. For this reason, Rybolovlev could not show the financial damage caused by Bouvier. But because of the scandal with Rybolovlev, Bouvier did lose a lot of money.

"When the problem with Rybolovlev began," Bouvier recalled, "I lost 40% of the turnover of my company, which was engaged in logistics and transport. As for selling art, before the scandal, I had a turnover of about $500 million a year. Then that figure dropped to $5-10 million, and since 2016 it has been zero." And it is clear why: Rybolovlev's clients were afraid that their treasures stored in Bouvier's Freeports could be seized while the case was being investigated.

Rybolovlev threatened Bouvier's Freeports without any benefit to himself. However, Bouvier had to sell his Singapore Freeport a loss to a Chinese buyer.

Due to judicial investigations in Monaco, France, and Switzerland, Rybolovlev, who never obtained Monegasque citizenship, began to strengthen his position in the US in June 2018. He invested $500 million in Apple Tree Partners (APT), a venture capital firm specializing in life sciences[85]. APT has offices in New York, London, San Francisco and Cambridge, Massachusetts.

Rybolovlev became an investor in New Republic Pictures, a film production company founded in 2017 in Hollywood with "the backing of wealthy individuals' funds based in Monaco and Spain"—as New Republic founder Brian Oliver put it, without mentioning Russia or Rybolovlev.

The company's chairman and chief operating officer is Russian citizen Valery An, who has numerous ties to Rybolovlev's structures and businesses. In 2015-2016, An was the marketing director of Rybolovlev's football club AS Monaco. He was also a consultant to Alevo and his email address ended "@rigmora.com" and belonged to Rybolovlev's family office Rigmora Holdings.

In August 2020, New Republic struck a deal worth more than $200 million with Paramount Pictures to finance up to a quarter of the budget of 10 films, including "Top Gun: Maverick" and "Mission Impossible—7. Part I," which for the first time for such a genre of films lacked a negative portrayal of Russia.

Here's what Bouvier had to say in an interview with entertainment investigative journalist Stacey Pearman:

"I know that Rybolovlev has been active in Hollywood since at least 2013. That year he asked me to get him tickets to Cannes Film Festival. He was not happy because they were not in the front row. He said, if I had asked my friends in Hollywood I would have been in the front row. I believe he entered Hollywood to advance the Kremlin agenda. Just look at Top Gun. The first film made it clear the enemy was Russia. They were fighting Migs flown by pilots with the soviet red star on their helmets. But in *Top Gun: Maverick* there is no reference to Russia at all and the enemy is deliberately ambiguous. I cannot believe this is by chance. I believe it is intimately linked to the fact the film was funded by a Russian oligarch. ...This is exactly what Russia is doing and fits with its broader hybrid warfare efforts in the West. We deserve to know exactly how much control funders and producers like Rybolovlev have over the creative decisions made in these films. There may be other examples of films funded by Rybolovlev where this has happened."

As soon as word leaked to the press that Rybolovlev and Russian money were involved in the production of the films, Valery An removed mention of AS Monaco from his online biography to hide his connection to Rybolovlev.

One can only guess how exactly Rybolovlev negotiated in the Kremlin and Lubyanka for permission to invest Trutnev's and Ezubchenko's money in Hollywood films.

On 20 November 2023, Rybolovlev and Bouvier's lawyers informed the Geneva prosecutor's office that they had reached an agreement and were withdrawing their criminal complaints from the courts. On 6 December, the prosecutor's office closed the last formally pending case against Bouvier. The Prosecutor's office reported that they were "unable to find any evidence to raise sufficient suspicion against" Bouvier. However, the procedural costs of CHF 100.000 were charged to Bouvier.

On 8 December 2023, Bouvier and Rybolovlev publicly announced that they had reached an amicable settlement and were dropping their mutual claims.

"Today marks the end of a nine-year nightmare. Courts all around the world have now unanimously concluded that I was innocent," Bouvier commented on the agreement. One of Bouvier's lawyers, David Bitton, added: "All the allegations against Mr. Bouvier were set aside by prosecutors around the world, and not a single court agreed to open a proper trial to review the accusations. This is a complete victory for my client. I want to thank all the lawyers throughout the world who stubbornly fought for justice and successfully defended the innocence of Mr. Bouvier."

"The parties have reached a confidential settlement concerning all their disputes that involved proceedings in various jurisdictions. They have no claims against each other and will refrain from commenting on their past disputes," Swiss lawyers for Rybolovlev, Sandrine Giroux and Benoit Mauron, said in her statement.

"As a person, Rybolovlev is ruthless," Bouvier said of him earlier. "He lacks emotion and is the most cynical person I have ever met. He has no friends. He doesn't care about friendship, human rights, the rule of law, the truth. He only cares about getting what he wants. He is almost a caricature of the typical Russian oligarch. He always thinks he is the smartest person in the room. He would try to tell a doctor the right way to cure a disease, or an artist how to paint. He is just as ruthless as a businessman. After his attacks against me, I conducted research and hired private investigators. It seems that throughout his career, Rybolovlev had been involved in many corrupt and criminal activities. I did not know that before, unfortunately. He seems to have worked with organized crime and local politicians to build his major fertilizer business, the source of his immense wealth. Since moving to the West, he has exported Russian techniques. He has systematically undermined the rule of law in every single market he operates… He corrupted the entire Monegasque judiciary to have me unlawfully arrested in Monaco… As long as he is not cornered—it is not in his character to settle. Like many other oligarchs, he doesn't want to show weakness... He doesn't want to give up his position under pressure. He will never change his mind... Rybolovlev believes that he dictates the laws, and he also sets the terms. And if at some point he concludes a truce or a peace agreement—it means that he simply had no choice."

Bouvier demanded €2 billion in damages from Rybolovlev, as the charges brought by Rybolovlev destroyed Bouvier's reputation and international business. Whether and what compensation he received from Rybolovlev remains a mystery.

A few weeks later on 30 January 2024, the trial of Dmitry Rybolovlev against Sotheby's auction house in New York also "was put to rest after the jury decided in favor of Sotheby's" and "jury found that the auction house was not responsible for aiding Yves Bouvier, a Swiss art dealer, in defrauding Rybolovlev of millions of dollars."[86]

At the end of 2023, Dmitry Rybolovlev's fortune was estimated by Forbes magazine at £8,74 billion. Over the 2023 calendar year, despite the war in Ukraine and the sanctions imposed on many Russian oligarchs and businesses (which Rybolovlev himself, unlike Trutnev, was not subject to), he increased his fortune by £513 million.

As for Donald Trump, his court cases will never end and he will spend years feeding lawyers, as Rybolovlev and Bouvier did before. But he is once again the Republican candidate. From the Kremlin's point of view, he is the most desirable candidate. It is no coincidence that former Russian President Dmitry Medvedev publicly called Trump "Colonel Daniil Fedorovich Trump,"[87] ready to surrender Ukraine, NATO and Europe to Putin, and turn America itself into another island of Cyprus[88].

Epilogue

1 https://www.theguardian.com/artanddesign/2017/dec/07/world-record-da-vinci-painting-to-be-exhibited-at-louvre-abu-dhabi

2 FD was the abbreviation for the Financial House (in Russian: *Finansovyi dom*).

3 https://haqqin.az/news/113183

4 https://publizist.ru/blogs/120626/46332/-; https://adpass.ru/vsya-kremlevskaya-rat-v-upravlenii-prezidenta-rf-po-vnutren-nej-politike-naznachen-novyj-zamestitel/

5 https://www.novayagazeta.ru/articles/2016/10/16/70202-vyshli-dengi-iz-provala

6 https://www.novayagazeta.ru/articles/2016/10/16/70202-vyshli-dengi-iz-provala

7 https://www.politico.com/magazine/story/2017/11/19/trump-first-moscow-trip-215842

8 https://www.kommersant.ru/doc/901088

9 https://www.washingtonpost.com/opinions/trump-loves-vladimir-putin-could-his-tax-returns-explain-why/2016/09/12/fe797fb0-7923-11e6-beac-57a4a412e93a_story.html?utm_term=.c4af6ea2d22f

10 https://www.kommersant.ru/doc/901088

11 http://www.motherjones.com/wp-content/uploads/millian-trump-630.jpg Millian is the person on the left of this photo.

12 http://www.motherjones.com/politics/2017/01/donald-trump-russia-sergei-millian/

13 https://www.wsj.com/articles/key-claims-in-trump-dossier-came-from-head-of-russian-american-business-group-source-1485253804

14 https://www.rospres.org/specserv/19992/

15 https://www.propublica.org/article/the-international-man-of-mystery-linked-to-flynns-lobbying-deal

16 http://ania.com/2017/05/19/exclusive-female-ex-russian-spy-appointed-trump-organization-launder-money/

17 https://www.wsj.com/articles/when-donald-trump-needs-a-loan-he-chooses-deutsche-bank-1458379806

18 https://www.nytimes.com/2017/01/16/us/politics/donald-trump-russia-business.html

19 For a concise list, see: https://en.wikipedia.org/wiki/Business_projects_of_Donald_Trump_in_Russia.

20 *Kommersant*, June 4, 2008, # 95.

21 https://chernovik.net/content/blogs/evgeniy-korotkovskiy/33-neschastya-kaliynogo-korolya-v-borbe-za-tron-kaliynogo-korolya

22 http://www.palmbeachdailynews.com/business/real-estate/trump-former-estate-the-story-behind-the-million-mansion-tear-down/5qgtlikl46SX7KXGdtDPUI/; http://www.tampabay.com/news/politics/why-did-russian-oligarch-pay-so-much-for-mansion-owned-by-trump/2316032

23 https://www.theguardian.com/world/2008/jul/17/donaldtrump.usa

24 https://www.bizjournals.com/southflorida/news/2017/10/06/russian-billionaire-makes-37m-selling-palm-beach.html

25 https://www.washingtonpost.com/news/fact-checker/wp/2016/07/27/trumps-claim-that-i-have-nothing-to-do-with-russia/?utm_term=.3ec78d41d237;
http://www.businessinsider.com/donald-trump-jr-said-money-pouring-in-from-russia-2018-2

26 https://www.msnbc.com/transcripts/transcript-rachel-maddow-show-december-24-2020-n1260862

27 http://gordonua.com/publications/pole-chudes-v-strane-durakov-tramp-v-pogone-za-russkimi-dengami-rassledovanie-istori-ka-felshtinskogo-230326.html

28 https://www.nytimes.com/2017/08/28/us/politics/trump-tower-putin-felix-sater.html

29 https://www.washingtonpost.com/blogs/the-fix/post/donald-trump-wont-run-for-president-in-2012/2011/05/16/AF14G14G_blog.html?utm_term=.ed22e29dd1bf

30 http://money.cnn.com/2013/01/23/news/companies/trump-new-york-times/index.html; http://www.businessinsider.com/donald-trump-is-trying-to-buy-the-new-york-times-2013-1

31 https://www.cnn.com/2017/07/12/politics/video-trump-relationships-russian-associates/index.html

32 https://twitter.com/realdonaldtrump/status/347191326112112640?lang=en

33 https://www.motherjones.com/politics/2018/05/new-documents-trump-pushed-hard-for-a-meeting-with-putin-in-2013/

34 http://www.chicagotribune.com/news/nationworld/politics/ct-trump-putin-invitiation-miss-universe-20180309-story.html

35 http://www.cnn.com/interactive/2017/03/politics/trump-putin-russia-timeline/

36 https://www.nbcnews.com/news/us-news/trump-putin-tried-meet-moscow-three-years-ago-source-n619006

37 http://www.newsweek.com/heres-all-times-trump-has-praised-putin-708859

38 http://rew-online.com/2013/11/12/hotel-trio-aims-to-bring-manhattan-to-moscow/

39 In January 2016 (as reported by the *Washington Post* on 28 August 2017), at the request of Felix Sater who worked as an intermediary on the deal, Michael Cohen contacted President Putin directly (through an email to his press secretary, Dmitry Peskov). Sater suggested contacting Putin because, according to him, the planned massive real estate development in Moscow by Trump would require the Russian Government's approval. In his email to Peskov, Cohen wrote, among other things, the following: "Over the past few months, I have been working with a company based in Russia regarding the development of a Trump Tower-Moscow project in Moscow City. Without getting into lengthy specifics, the communication between our two sides has stalled. As this project is very important, I am hereby requesting your assistance. I respectfully request someone, preferably you, contact me so that I might discuss the specifics as well as arrange meetings with the appropriate individuals. I thank you in advance for your assistance and look forward to hearing from you soon."

40 Many other prominent Russian businessmen were clients of Neocleous' law firm. Neocleous and his children have long been known as people who specialize in managing the offshore business of influential Russian businessmen. Neocleous Sr. came to Russia in the early 1990s or even earlier and established his law firm in Moscow. The Neocleous family company managed clients' offshore networks, controlling not only Cyprus offshore, but also working with the Virgin Islands and Seychelles. Andreas Neocleous stepped back from running the firm at some point, leaving his son Elias in charge of the business. For Rybolovlev, Neocleous created, among other things, the family trusts "Aries" and "Virgo", named after the zodiac signs of his two daughters, and a network of companies registered in tax havens controlled by the trusts in Cyprus, where Rybolovlev and his partners' money was kept.

41 That's also where Cypriot President Nicos Anastasiades and his wife Andri were due to arrive on Rybolovlev's plane. At the last moment, Anastasiades refused to go to the lavish party, as it would have been badly received by Cypriots, whose country was going through a financial crisis at the time. Only Andri flew to the birthday party.

42 Sartori was born on 6 February 1981 in Uruguay. He moved to Switzerland in 1993. On 21 October 2015, he became the husband of Ekaterina Rybolovleva.

43 https://versia.ru/kak-yeks-vladelec-uralkaliya-dmitrij-rybolovlev-ogorchil-princa-monako-i-vnov-zastavil-volnovatsya-vip-vkladchikov-vneshprombanka

44 https://www.townandcountrymag.com/society/money-and-power/a4327/billionaire-defrauded-art-world-scheme/

45 In January 2013, Vasiliev joined Rybolovlev as an advisor on the presidency of AS Monaco Football Club. He was subsequently asked to join the club permanently and on 25 March 2013, he became sporting director, managing the first team, player recruitment, scouting, coaching staff, and medical service. In August 2013, he became vice-president. After a disappointing 2018-2019 season for the team, Vasiliev was sacked by Rybolovlev in February 2019 and Rybolovlev himself became vice-president and CEO of AS Monaco.

46 https://www.kp.ru/daily/27445.3/4647026/

47 https://www.newyorker.com/magazine/2016/02/08/the-bouvier-affair

48 See French journalist Renaud Revel's e-book *Le mystérieux Monsieur Rybolovlev* (2017), chapter *The King of Cyprus*.

49 It is being published this year (2024) by the publishing house Alfadi (Cyprus).

50 https://www.theguardian.com/business/2017/jan/31/deutsche-bank-fined-630m-over-russia-money-laundering-claims; (http://money.cnn.com/2017/01/31/investing/deutsche-bank-us-fine-russia-money-laundering/index.html

51 Rybolovlev "befriended" the Cypriot president during all the years of his rule, although his meetings with him were mostly secret: they met in German hotels, in some clinics where they happened to meet "by chance" at the same time, and even in Dublin (on 6 March 2014, where Cypriot President Nicos Anastasiades attended the congress of the European People's Party).

52 The fact that Rybolovlev paid for the aircraft of the president was concealed from the Greek and international public when this was possible. For example, on 8 June 2014, when Anastasiades traveled to Egypt to attend the swearing-in of President Abdel Fattah al-Sisi, he used a private jet chartered by an Egyptian company. On 12 June, Anastasiades hosted a

dinner at the presidential palace for Cypriot businessman Chris Lazari from London. After the meal, Chris Lazari issued a statement saying that he would bear the cost of renting private jets for the president when circumstances require it. Lazari clarified that he does not do business in Cyprus and is solely motivated by his long-standing friendship with the president. Immediately afterward, Anastasiades issued his statement, thanking Lazari for his "generous gesture and for his selfless support to the Government's efforts, as well as his efforts, to achieve the best for our country." On 25 June, Anastasiades traveled to Brussels to attend the EU Council meeting. He traveled on the same plane to Egypt for al-Sisi's swearing-in ceremony. Also in the entourage were the special adviser to the president of the Republic of Cyprus Makarios Drousiotis, and the new presidential spokesman, Nicos Christodoulides. "God bless Lazari, we're flying on a jet..." Drousiotis pronounced as a plane took off. "You mean Rybolovlev," Christodoulides replied. Lazaris' gift was a screen: he never paid for Anastasiades' flights.

53 When the Rybolovlev Law was passed, Averof Neophytou strongly opposed to it in parliament, arguing that the proposed amendments were "provocatively incompatible" with the EU acquis. "It is shameful that European Cyprus is writing up tailor-made legislative proposals to serve the interests of perhaps only one client, disregarding the possible damage to our country's credibility and interest," he said and demanded that the "Rybolovlev Law" be sent to the EU to see if the bill is compatible with EU norms. Rybolovlev drew the "right conclusion" from what was happening, and after the passage of the "Rybolovlev Law" (in defiance of Neophyte's opposition) hired him as his lawyer, thus ensuring his support in future legislative battles.

54 In effect, judging from Bersheda's later published texts, he was an intermediary between Rybolovlev and Cypriot politicians, and in particular between Rybolovlev and Anastasiades.

55 On corruption in Cypress see also: https://www.occrp.org/en/daily/18488-cyprus-to-probe-graft-allegations-against-former-president-nicos-anastasiades https://in-cyprus.philenews.com/local/anastasiades-corruption-probe-focuses-on-surveillance-claims-in-mafia-state/ https://www.euractiv.com/section/media/news/whistleblower-spyware-helps-the-mafia-rule-in-cyprus/

56 Elena Rybolovleva's attempts to seize her husband's property and Dmitry Rybolovlev's corresponding counter-attempts to lift the seizure of her property were numerous, starting on 29 December 2008, when she filed her first application for a provisional worldwide seizure of her husband's property, but was refused on 31 August 2009. On 4 March 2010, the refusal was overturned by the court and the provisional seizure was approved. On 6 April 2010, Rybolovlev filed an appeal, but the appeal was rejected on 27 April 2010. On 26 April 2012 Rybolovlev again sought to overturn the Swiss court's ruling, but on 22 May 2012 his request was again rejected, although this in practice applied only to Switzerland and not to Singapore, London, Monaco or Cyprus.

57 https://www.eureporter.co/world/russia/2021/09/20/yves-bouvier-fully-cleared-of-all-charges-in-his-dispute-against-russia-oligarch-dmitry-rybolovlev/#google_vignette; https://news.artnet.com/art-world/yves-bouvier-declares-total-victory-dmitry-rybolovlev-2010315

58 https://www.bloomberg.com/news/features/2017-02-23/a-100-million-mystery-a-russian-his-art-and-his-big-losses

59 https://www.bloomberg.com/news/articles/2017-03-07/russian-billionaire-loses-150-million-on-sale-of-four-artworks

60 https://www.artmarketmonitor.com/2017/02/23/in-a-hurry-to-put-his-bad-deals-behind-him-rybolovlev-sells-at-a-loss/

61 It was due to these bright prospects that Trutnev retained his position in the new government formed by Putin after he won the Presidential election again in March 2018.

62 http://www.kremlin.ru/events/president/news/47173

63 https://ru.wikipedia.org/wiki/%D0%A1%D0%B2%D0%BE%D0%B1%D0%BE%D0%B4%D0%BD%D1%8B%D0%B9_%D0%BF%D0%BE%D1%80%D1%82_%D0%92%D0%BB%D0%B0%D0%B4%D0%B8%D0%B2%D0%BE%D1%81%D1%82%D0%BE%D0%BA

64 https://static1.squarespace.com/static/59f8f41ef14aa13b95239af0/t/608951716e2ea938a469b9b3/1619612099434/Kremligarchs.pdf

65 Alexander Osipov started his career as a "tax inspector" in 1991, although he was still a student. In 1991, the Russian tax service was under the jurisdiction of the KGB. He later became an expert on energy investments and was CFO of the energy company Itera, whose founder, Igor Makarov, hired Semyon Mogilevich, a member of the Russian security services and a known criminal mastermind, as his head of security. In 2018, Putin appointed Osipov as governor of the Trans-Baikal Territory.

66 Alexei Chekunkov was the CEO of the Far East Development Fund, part of the Far East Development Ministry, and a member of Alrosa's Strategic Planning Committee. Chekunkov graduated from the MGIMO Institute, which is closely associated with special services. He was an informal adviser to high-ranking Kremlin officials on investment issues in Russia and abroad.

67 https://www.gq.ru/person/kak-ustroen-almaznyj-biznes-v-rossii

68 https://www.gq.ru/person/kak-ustroen-almaznyj-biznes-v-rossii

69 https://www.huffingtonpost.com/entry/shuttle-election-diplomacy-dmitry-rybolovlevs-plane_us_58a7651ae4b026a89a7a2acb

70 http://www.palmerreport.com/opinion/dmitry-rybolovlevs-flight-patterns-suggests-played-role-trump-russia-blackmail-

negotiations/1809/

71 https://www.theguardian.com/world/2017/oct/19/russian-scrutinised-for-ties-to-trump-investigated-in-monaco

72 https://www.huffingtonpost.com/entry/shuttle-election-diplomacy-dmitry-rybolovlevs-plane_us_58a7651ae4b026a89a7a2acb

73 https://www.mypalmbeachpost.com/news/national-govt---politics/from-2017-yachts-trump-financial-backer-russian-oligarch-seen-close-together/gI074W3JLqvEYrQ0hm9zlN/

74 As Commerce Secretary, Ross did not divest his financial stakes in several organizations, as he pledged to do in November 2017 before the US Office of Government Ethics. These included stakes in Bank of Cyprus and Navigator Holding, as well as companies co-owned by the Chinese government. Ross owned stakes in Navigator Holdings through a chain of offshore investments. Navigator was involved in transporting petrochemical products for Russia's Sibur, which was sanctioned in the United States for ties to Russian oligarchs Leonid Mikhelson, Gennady Timchenko, and Kirill Shalamov, Putin's former son-in-law.

75 https://www.bizjournals.com/charlotte/news/2017/02/28/alevo-gets-incentives-worth-13-2m-to-expand.html

76 http://www.mcclatchydc.com/news/nation-world/national/article141308758.html

77 Vladislav Baumgertner, born in 1972, was Uralkali's commercial director between 2003 and 2005, then served as the company's CEO until 2013. In August 2013, after Uralkali was sold to Kerimov, Baumgertner was arrested in Belarus for abuse of office and causing damage to the Belarusian Potash Company and Belaruskali totaling more than $100 million. Kerimov, fighting to increase Uralkali's share of the potash market, organized a price dumping war, which led to a drop in global potash prices and nearly bankrupted Kerimov's Belarusian partner, who was Lukashenko. Lukashenko then lured Baumgertner to Minsk under the pretext of negotiations and took him hostage. Baumgertner was convicted by a Minsk court for abuse of office and sentenced to two months in prison followed by three months in custody at his home before being extradited to Russia under house arrest. It took Rybolovlev's intervention for him to be released from house arrest on bail in September 2014 and the charges against him were dropped on 23 February 2015. https://www.forbes.ru/kompanii/resursy/247712-voennoplennyi-kak-vladislav-baumgertner-stal-zalozhnikom-aleksandra-lukashen

78 Petrov had already left the company in August 2017, when the company filed for bankruptcy. Baumgertner and other Rybolovlev employees left Alevo in October.

79 http://www.charlotteobserver.com/news/business/article167970747.html

80 https://www.aljazeera.com/news/2017/05/trump-arrives-saudi-arabia-foreign-trip-170520063253596.html

81 https://www.whitehouse.gov/briefings-statements/remarks-president-trump-crown-prince-mohammed-bin-salman-kingdom-saudi-arabia-bilateral-meeting/

82 https://www.bloomberg.com/news/articles/2017-10-19/russian-owner-of-as-monaco-charged-over-privacy-invasion-claim

83 http://www.monacomatin.mc/amp/justice/lancien-procureur-de-monaco-jean-pierre-dreno-inculpe-237782

84 https://www.bloomberg.com/news/articles/2018-05-29/russian-s-da-vinci-windfall-undercut-u-s-probe-of-art-dealer

85 https://thebell.io/rybolovlev-ne-poboyalsya-sanktsij-milliarder-vlozhil-svyshe-500-mln-v-amerikanskie-startapy/

86 https://itsartlaw.org/2024/02/15/diversity-fraud-accent-delight-v-sothebys/ Rybolovlev tried to attack Bouvier in 9 different jurisdictions and lost everywhere. The final criminal investigation against Bouvier was closed by the Geneva Public Prosecutor's Office in December 2023. Rybolovlev, on his end, got indicted in Monaco, Switzerland and France for the activities he conducted against Bouvier.

87 https://t.me/medvedev_telegram, 18 March 2023.

88 https://dossier-center.appspot.com/cyprus/

Printed in the USA
CPSIA information can be obtained
at www.ICGtesting.com
JSHW040748300724
67277JS00004B/7